CHRISTOPHER
COLUMBUS

LOUIS MACNEICE

CHRISTOPHER COLUMBUS

a radio play

FABER & FABER

First published in Mcmxliv
by Faber and Faber Limited
24 Russell Square London W.C. 1
Second impression April Mcmxliv
Third impression November Mcmxlix
Fourth impression July Mcmliii
Fifth impression April Mcmliv
Sixth impression March Mcmlxi
Printed in Great Britain by
Lowe & Brydone (Printers) Ltd
London N.W. 10

44-4602

CAST

in the order of their appearance

The first performance of the radio play was given by the B.B.C. on the 12th October, 1942, in the Home Service.

THE VOICE OF DOUBT	*Robert Speaight*
THE VOICE OF FAITH	*Marius Goring*
JOSÉ	*Philip Cunningham*
ARTUR	*Harry Hutchinson*
ALFREDO	*Mark Dignam*
BARTOLOMÉ	*Stephen Murray*
CARLOS	*Jack Livesey*
FRANCISCO	*Alan Wheatley*
BROTHER PEDRO	*Bryan Powley*
PRIOR	*Arthur Young*
COLUMBUS	*Laurence Olivier*
ANTONIO	*Allan Jeayes*
THE HERALD	*Marius Goring*
TALAVERA	*Cecil Trouncer*
MEDINA–CELI	*John Bryning*
MEDINA–SIDONIA	*Robert Rendel*
MENDOZA	*Lawrence Hanray*
1ST LACKEY	*Peter Cotes*
2ND LACKEY	*Grey Blake*
MARQUESA	*Hedli Anderson*
QUEEN ISABELLA	*Gladys Young*
DIEGO DE DEZA	*Alexander Sarner*
MANUEL	*Jonathan Field*
TAPSTRESS	*Molly Rankin*
JUAN	*Stuart Latham*
BEATRIZ	*Margaret Rawlings*
A WAITING WOMAN	*Lucille Lisle*
OBSERVER	*Robert Speaight*
VASCO	*Frederick Burtwell*
LUIS	*Ralph Roberts*
A TOWN CRIER	*Richard George*
MARTÍN PINZÓN	*Richard Williams*

[5]

74987

CAST

A STOREKEEPER	*Philip Cunningham*
A SERVANT	*Jonathan Field*
A SAILOR'S VOICE 1	*Grey Blake*
A SAILOR'S VOICE 2	*Robert Rendel*
MATE	*Bryan Powley*
A WOMAN	*Lucille Lisle*
SPOKESMAN OF CREW	*William Trent*
GUTIÉRREZ	*Laidman Browne*
SÁNCHEZ	*Harry Hutchinson*
VICENTE PINZÓN	*Richard George*
ESCOVEDO	*John Bryning*
SEGOVIA	*Lawrence Hanray*
HIDALGO	*Mark Dignam*
A PEASANT	*Jonathan Field*
A CLERIC	*Peter Cotes*
AN ONLOOKER	*Robert Speaight*
SPOKESMAN OF THE PROCESSION	*Marius Goring*

Others taking part were the B.B.C. Symphony Orchestra and the B.B.C. Chorus (under Chorus-master Leslie Woodgate) conducted by Sir Adrian Boult. Also the solo singers Joan Lennard, Bradbridge White and Stanley Riley, and the guitarist George Elliott. The music was specially composed by William Walton.

The programme was produced by Dallas Bower.

Lack of Acknowledgments

Both before performance on the air and before publication various authorities on Spain and Spanish history very kindly vetted my text. For this I am most grateful to them but I am not printing their names here as, while taking some of their advice, I also ignored a good deal of it, and I do not wish my wilfulness laid, by any chance, at their door.

INTRODUCTION

SOME COMMENTS ON RADIO DRAMA

(i)
Apologia

After deciding to publish this radio play I was asked to write an introduction to it and I suppose that, if one is worth doing, so is the other; the book-buying public is still very ignorant of radio. Radio plays and 'features' (dramatic documentaries), when laid on the printed page, tend to lose even more than do plays written for the theatre. But *Christopher Columbus* is something of a special case in that it is unusually long and is written throughout in a more or less stylised form and with comparatively long sequences (scenes) which therefore make less demands on a reader's imagination. I am having it published not only because I hope that it will be readable but because it may interest some members of the more literary public in a popular art-form which still is an art-form. In the following pages I shall talk about radio-dramatic writing. My generalisations, like all generalisations, will be only approximately true and will be coloured by personal bias.

In the following pages I do not attempt to do justice to the more topical species of radio documentary. This species is large and elastic and, at its best, can compete with the best journalism (or cinema news-reel) and the best short-stories (or topical story-films). This species has enormous possibilities but these are outside the scope of this introduction. I am limiting my attention to that kind of radio-dramatic writing—historical or imaginative—which might loosely be called 'creative'.

(ii)
Requirements of the Medium

'Creative' works written for broadcasting, while having a vastly larger public than stage-plays, novels or poetry, get, in the ordinary sense, very much less publicity. They are heard once and no one has a chance to go back to them. Only a few periodicals carry radio critiques and these are sometimes written by persons

[7]

who have not fully taken in the aims and limitations of the medium. If you cannot enjoy the spoken word with your eyes shut, don't try to criticise radio.

✓ Sound-broadcasting gets its effects through sound and sound alone. This very obvious fact has two somewhat contradictory implications: (1) A good radio play or feature presupposes a good radio script; (2) such a script is not necessarily a piece of 'good writing'.

This second point needs amplifying. The good writer who writes only for the page concerns himself with words alone; the radio writer has to think of *words in the mouths of actors*.[1] Consequently those subtleties which the ordinary writer uses in rhythm or phrasing—or thought—will often be superfluous and sometimes detrimental to the radio writer. An analogy (apart from the legitimate stage, where, thanks to visual compensations, a playwright can often get away with literary excrescences) can be found in the writing of lyrics for music; if you write a lyric to be set it is in most cases unnecessary, if not indeed injurious, to employ to any extent the more fancy tricks of prosody; your significant variations of rhythm, your internal rhymes, your off-rhymes and assonances and technical surprises, will get in the composer's way; it is *his* job to add the significant variations.

This subordination in radio of words to words-as-they-are-spoken has for the writer both its regrets and its rewards. He may have to lay aside some of his technical equipment but, provided his piece is well produced, he can count on his words regaining those literary virtues which literature itself has lost since it has been divorced from the voice. He can for example write the same line five times to achieve five different effects. Or he can write deliberately flat, understate, with the knowledge that this understatement will be heightened as required by the voice. The voice too will help him to squeeze from a cliché that expressiveness which many clichés still retain. These possibilities, I feel, should be peculiarly welcome to many contemporary writers. With a literature so old as ours and a contemporary diction so vulgarised, precise and emotive writing comes to depend more and more upon twists—twists of the obvious statement or the hackneyed image. To do this on the printed page requires constant ingenuity and often leads to an appearance of being too clever by half. In radio,

[1] The term 'actors' is to be taken to include persons from real life enacting themselves.

without sacrificing simplicity or lucidity, you can often leave the twisting to the voice. But while being thus indebted to the voice for special effects, you must never attempt effects which voices cannot procure. Your trade is in words-as-they-are-spoken—and words-as-they-are-heard.

(iii)
Requirements of the Audience

The radio writer is not only limited by his medium; he is also limited by his audience. This audience, which should be reckoned in millions,[1] is under no obligation to listen to him. The writer therefore must make his work, if not intelligible, at least interesting to the millions. This in general precludes an esoteric content or manner, an obviously highbrow approach, or anything which puts too great a strain on a simple man sitting by his fireside.

This synthetic figure of the Ordinary Listener tends to become a bugbear to radio writers and producers; it would be very natural to draw the inference that to hold the attention of this listener a writer has got to 'write down'. (By writing down I mean pandering—writing by standards which the writer considers low.) This inference would be false. Radio writing must, in the majority of cases, be popular; it need not ever be vulgar. The argument for its vulgarity rests on a misconception of our old friend, the Man-in-the-Street.

I admit that the man-in-the-street cannot be assumed to have much intellectual apparatus and is not as a rule prepared to make great intellectual efforts. That is why he cannot cope with the higher sciences or philosophy. But radio-drama—like the other forms of drama—is not a higher science; it appeals to the emotions rather than to the reason and requires a sensitive more than an educated audience. In making this distinction I do not forget that aesthetic sensibility can be developed by education but I refuse to believe that men and women in the street are as insensitive or as emotionally atrophied as is sometimes assumed by the intelligentsia. The trouble with 'ordinary people' is not that they have innately bad taste but that they can be easily conditioned to admire

[1] While I am in favour of occasional special programmes for small minority audiences, radio as an institution is, like the cinema, obliged on the whole to envisage a regular public large enough to keep the radio business going.

what is vulgar and emotionally false. Give them a year of the Wurlitzer Organ and they will not stomach a symphony orchestra. Write down to them and they will never look up.

If then the radio writer must not write down, how is he to get on terms with this unseen audience which is so easily bored, so attuned to bad art, so unconscious that it is an audience? I would answer that the first thing he must do is to forget about 'literature' and to concentrate upon sound (see section viii). This is not to deny literature, for this is how literature began—the Homeric or Icelandic bard shouting over the clamour of the banquet, the 'tale told in a chimney corner' while tankards clatter and infants squawl and somebody makes up the fire and old men snore and cough. The radio listener listens in a terribly every-day setting; there is no auditorium to beglamour him and predispose him to accept you; if you want him to accept you, you will have to seduce him by sound and sound alone. But seduction is a necessary part of many human relationships and here, as elsewhere, can be achieved without either lies or crudity.

(iv)
Radio-Drama and Poetry

All the arts, to varying degrees, involve some kind of a compromise. This being so, how far need the radio dramatist go to meet the public without losing sight of himself and his own standards of value? He obviously cannot aspire to the freedom of lyric poetry written for the page; he must work to the limitations, already described, imposed both by medium and audience. This audience he must regard, if only because of its size and diversity, as a primitive one; to reach it he must move on a more or less primitive plane. But what is primitive is not *ipso facto* crude or false or childish or even outmoded. This plane precludes the higher mathematics and the more erudite *nuances* of symbolist poetry; it does not preclude the basic human emotions or their broader forms of expression. It does not therefore preclude the broader forms of poetry.

For man, we should always remember, is born poetic. Hence the predominance of nursery rhymes in the nursery and of poetry in all early literatures. Poetry, in this one sense at least, is more primitive than prose; it was easier on the ear and less strain upon the mind. That is why radio drama—not because the medium is new but because of its primitive audience—might reasonably be expected to demand a poet's approach. And poets on the whole do seem more at home on the air than novelists, say, or essayists. But the modern public, we shall be told, is not at home to poetry. This I do not believe. The man-in-the-street who admires Walt Disney, is not a scientific 'realist'; he is ready to welcome certain forms of design, rhythm and fantasy. He may dislike *the idea of poetry* but that is because he has been conditioned to think of poetry as something too sissy, infantile, difficult or irrelevant. Thus the mere sight of verse on the page (like a menu printed in French) is enough to frighten him off. Verse, however, when coming out of his radio set, will not strike him—at least not too aggressively—as *verse*; instead of prejudging it as a piece of high-brow trickery he will, like the audience of the primitive bards, listen to the words, or rather to the sounds, as they come and will like them or not according to their emotional impact. Since the defence mechanism of his prejudices is suspended, this impact may often be surprisingly weighty.

When I spoke above of a 'poet's approach' I did not mean this narrowly in the sense of versification (see the next section and section vii) but it is worth stressing the point that it is fairly easy to get away with verse on the air. Write a piece of dialogue or narra-tion in an obviously rhythmical but not too strait-laced verse-form and the radio audience will accept it, thinking of it probably as just a powerful bit of language. The academic listener on the other hand—not that academics often listen—will find himself in an unusually normal position; not having a printed page to ponder and scan, he will be unable to decide by his eye that the poet's words have no rhythm and will have to allow his ear to admit what rhythms emerge.

(v)
Construction in Radio Drama

If radio drama is poetic, its poetry—like poetry in general—must consist of a great deal more than rhythmical patterns of words; it presupposes a wider and deeper pattern beginning with a careful and intuitive selection of material and culminating in a large architectonic. The first virtue of a radio script is construction.

A novel can legitimately be rambling and discursive, a narrative poem can be padded with decoration, a short story can be a chunk of impressions, Belles Lettres can be merely 'belles', but a radio play or feature must have a dramatic unity; in the jargon of the trade, it must have the proper 'builds' and an 'over-all' shape. It is as a builder in this sense that the radio dramatist, however prosaic or colloquial or dry his dialogue, is by his nature nearer to the poet than to the journalist.[1] This is true of 'features' as well as of plays. The radio feature is a dramatised presentation of actuality but its author should be much more than a *rapporteur* or a cameraman; he must select his actuality material with great discrimination and then keep control of it so that it subserves a single dramatic effect.

In achieving a dramatic unity the radio writer must, as a rule, be more economical than the playwright proper. For (1) he normally has a much narrower time-limit, usually from thirty to sixty minutes; (2) his speakers being invisible, he has to take many more pains to 'plant' his situations; (3) his audience having no visual aids to imagination or memory, he must be much more careful not to confuse them with sideshows or bore them with dull patches or strain their memory with references back—if there was just one key line you can never be sure that they caught it. Characters and situations must be clearly established and the line of development be strong and simple.

Yet, when you look at the theatre, you find you have your compensations. Provided you make clear your transitions from scene to scene, you can take many more liberties with time and place; you are free of the dead hand of the Three Act tradition. You can jump from India to the Arctic and from 1066 to 1943. You can make a point with a scene consisting of three lines and no one need fiddle with a curtain or black out the lights. And you can, with less fuss and more credibility than on the stage (and perhaps than on the screen), introduce—if you want to—allegorical speakers or choruses. You can again, with the help of music and recorded effects (but see section viii), present all sorts of scenes—especially scenes of action—that the theatre can rarely attempt. You can finally (though this applies mostly to features) get an effect, if you want to, of up-to-the-minute actuality, a set-piece as vivid as a running commentary. With all this you must

[1] The Greek derivation of 'poet', though hackneyed, is still worth remembering.

remember that you cannot compete in trappings or tricks with either the cinema or the theatre; your medium being sound alone, you must stand or fall by the use you make of words.

(vi)
Radio Craftsmanship

If the over-all planning of a radio drama needs a certain creative artistry, its detailed working-out needs craftsmanship. Radio is not a good channel for souls in flux, for the kind of inspiration that sings and does not count the cost. A radio writer must write to an exact scale, with every link made firm and no loose ends; he must not only, as I said, woo his audience cunningly; he must work to hold their interest; two or three minutes of even legitimate boredom may bring their hands to the knob that switches him off.

Another reason for craftsmanship is the fact that many radio scripts are, inevitably, commissioned work, and that the persons who commission such work must inevitably judge it by more or less professional standards. This is not to deny that it is the duty of any broadcasting institution to invite *spontaneous* contributions from 'outside writers'. It is merely to recognise the obvious fact that an organisation working on such a scale cannot depend entirely on spontaneity and must therefore partly rely upon such writers as are prepared to practise radio-writing as a *craft*. That this fact, though repugnant to some artists, is not incompatible with art, is proved by those many periods in history where the basis of the arts has been an accepted triangle—patron, professional artist and public. I do not suggest that this triangle is to be found at its best in the world of radio today; there are too many factors—commercial or bureaucratic—that confuse, hamper and vulgarise. One virtue, however, of radio's contemporary triangle is that it insists on a function of words which salon-writers are perhaps too apt to forget; this function is communication. The distinction of 'communication' from 'self-expression' is misleading. If compelled to communicate with a fair-sized public, a writer may sometimes find himself expressing bits of himself that he had lost.

To prevent misunderstanding, I should add that I do not hold that the writer's[1] chief job is to write for a majority public—let

[1] I am speaking here of the writer in general.

alone pander to it. There are many themes which can only be understood by a minority; there are certain treatments which only a minority will appreciate. To assert, as some do, that all art should have mass-appeal is like asserting that all mathematics should be 'for the million'. On the other hand, there *are* themes and treatments which the masses and the writer can enjoy in common. These are for the most part the same themes and treatments that have been ousted from the literary salon and abandoned to the films and the newspapers. A writer in reclaiming them is at the same time giving himself a tonic (a dose of earth and ozone) and helping to correct the public's taste. Such a reclamation is possible in radio which in spite of its many temptations to vulgarity, is at least more free from those temptations than either the press or the cinema.

(vii)
The Importance of 'Story'

What are these themes and treatments? The themes consist, roughly speaking, of anything that in a newspaper sense can be called a 'story'—the Trojan War, the Hound of the Baskervilles, the story of a penny, Elsie's week-end. The treatment, roughly speaking, will be broad, lucid and dramatic—dramatic in the Aristotelian sense that the central event, or theme, will be central and everything else, including characters, subordinate.[1] As compared with most contemporary literature, the objective elements will preponderate over the subjective, statement over allusion, synthesis over analysis. We are at a far remove not only from Proust or Joyce but also from Shaw's conversation plays and the middle-brow 'psychological' novel.

Writers of my generation, brought up on chunks of life and the stream of consciousness, must often have envied the old-fashioned story-teller—or the modern writer of detective fiction—this element of plot, of simple progression from event to event. But stories in themselves—*contes, Märchen, muthoi* or what-have-you— being essentially primitive, had become as suspect to many modern writers as the literary element in painting had to many modern painters. This was partly because his background tends to make the modern writer an introvert and partly because at this stage of

[1] Compare the remarks of W. B. Yeats on Tragedy.

[14]

our literature there already was a glut of books which relied chiefly on story. Now however our background is changing and forcing us again to take an interest in what people *do*. And, if we want to present what they do, we can still avoid the staleness of the printed word by resorting to other media; and one of these is radio. I for one, having always preferred the Icelandic sagas to the modern novel, am only too pleased to discover that a medium exists where a saga treatment is still feasible.

An early and excellent example of a popular story treated broadly, rapidly and vividly with all the resources of radio was *The March of the '45* by D. G. Bridson (first transmitted by the B.B.C. in 1936). This programme followed Prince Charles Edward from his landing in the Hebrides to his final defeat at Culloden, peaking the action with bagpipes and Jacobite songs and covering the transitions with a quick-fire verse commentary skilfully varied in form to match the changes of mood. This achieved a total effect unattainable on the stage and less simply attainable on the screen. (Most film directors have yet to learn not to sow with the whole sack; the talking film still suffers from trying to do too much at once.)

Regular listeners to British radio will have noticed, at least in these recent war-years, a predominance of stories of the hot news variety. This was inevitable and it must be admitted that radio is an adequate medium for topical *rapportage* and realistic impressionism. But my own opinion is that the radio play (if not the radio feature) can only reach its heights when the subject is slightly larger, or at least simpler, than life and the treatment is to some extent stylised—when, we might say, it is competing with the Soviet art-cinema rather than with Hollywood or the standardised news-reel. I found this borne out in practice when I was asked to make a radio adaptation of Eisenstein's film *Alexander Nevsky*. This film, which disappointed some English intellectuals because of its lack of subtlety in characterisation, its complete innocence of psychological conflict, its primitive pattern of Black versus White, was for those very reasons easily transposed into a radio form, Prokofieff's incidental music which had been an integral part of the film helping equally in its turn to integrate the theme on the air.

(viii)
Radio Production

This mention of music brings me back to my main thesis that, while in radio drama words are of the utmost importance, the radio dramatist must think in terms of sound rather than of words alone. He must therefore be studio-conscious, remembering what results can and cannot be obtained from a limited number of microphones, a control panel and a gramophone turn-table. There are some veterans of broadcasting who go so far as to say that no radio script can be more than a very rough notation for the producer, a hunk of raw material which can only take on shape in transmission. This is an overstatement—a really good script should survive a bad production—but it is undeniable that to write a really good script you have to remember not only the microphone which is going to accept it but the loud-speaker, or rather the million loud-speakers, which are going to deliver it.

A surprising number of persons appear to be completely ignorant of *how* a radio 'show' gets on to the air: it is even sometimes assumed that a radio play or feature goes out without any rehearsal. For this reason I do not think it superfluous to add here a few remarks on production. If we leave aside the more technical but minor points of acoustic perspectives, of balance, fading etc., there are three ingredients, apart from the words themselves, which are of primary importance—voices, effects, and music.

(ix)
The Voices

The voices of radio actors come in for a lot of criticism, much of it justifiable but some of it unjust. It must be remembered, in comparison with the theatre, that the radio actor, because he is not seen, is at a double disadvantage; he has to rely solely on his voice both to establish himself as a genuine character and to distinguish himself from the rest of the cast. On the whole, actors on the air probably use a less phoney delivery than actors on the stage, but the grease-paint voice will stick out all the more when there is no real grease-paint to look at and when the listener, instead of being self-consciously seated on plush and transported out of reality by

[16]

coloured lights, is listening to dramatised speech in the too-too real context of his home. As for the differentiation of characters you can put twenty-one Oxford undergraduates on the stage, short and long, blond and black, all drawling away in the 'Oxford manner', but you cannot do that on the air without causing hopeless confusion.

In both these respects the writer can make things much easier for his cast. He must 'envisage' what kinds of voices will be heard together on the air and he must apportion the lines in such a way as to help any necessary contrast. Another very important point: remembering that much of the colour of radio is achieved by variations of tempo, he must avoid writing, as it were, by the metronome; taking a bird's-eye view of the needed contours of his programme he must undulate his scenes and the dialogue itself accordingly.

(x)
The 'Effects'

'Effects', in the sense of naturalistic noises contributing atmosphere or establishing a fact, are of two kinds—records on a gramophone or spot effects in the studio. The trouble is that they often sound what they are—that is, a put-up job. They are, however, sometimes necessary for reasons of vividness and economy. A cow mooing will call up a farmyard more quickly and more vividly than a paragraph of word-painting; all you need is a decent record of a cow. If there is only a bad recording available, it is better to word-paint or else to do a cow on the trombone. In my own opinion musical effects often can—and should—be substituted for naturalistic ones, though this is of course less feasible when a programme purports to be a direct transcript of actuality.

Those effects which one would most welcome are also too often those which least ring true. This is so with all noises that suggest enormous power and express this power by volume; on the air their volume disappears. A writer therefore should not, after building up to a battle, say, or a thunderstorm, rely upon mere effects to point the climax; *if* he must use these effects, he should frame them very carefully with words. And, as regards recorded effects (the notorious example is the B.B.C. sea-gull), he must remember that, as with some repertory actors, they may become much too familiar to the listening public and therefore defeat their own end and make the whole scene unreal. In general, a radio writer should only ask for effects when they are (*a*) practicable, (*b*) an asset to his story. They must not be overused nor indulged in for their own sake.

(xi)
The Music

The use of music in radio features and plays has always been, and remains, a subject of controversy. Like naturalistic effects, it has too often been inserted from the mere love of variation or the mere fear of boring the audience with long stretches of speech; there is no evidence, however, that the public is really so allergic to the naked word. What music can very often do is to compensate for the lack of the visual element, to establish an emotional atmosphere or to register a change of mood more vividly, and more quickly, than words alone. In radio it is used in two ways— (1) by itself, before, between or after the spoken passages, (2) as an atmospheric background to speech. In either case it should serve a functional purpose.

Music by itself is chiefly useful either as a link or to make an emotional peak. In a form which tends to involve many short sequences and therefore many transitions in space and time, an appropriate musical link will smooth over the transition and will often, in some cases, convey information less creakingly or cumbrously than words will; the impersonal Narrator who says 'And now we take you to August 1914' is a bore; it is preferable to play *Tipperary* (reinforced, if you like, with marching feet). Information can of course be given in another way by specially written music of the descriptive kind sometimes used on the films— music, that, like onomatopœic language, achieves a *similitude* in sound to the object described.

Radio's other use of music is as background to speech. This is often very messy. The ear finds it difficult to follow two things at once. In general I would say that background music should not be used for realistic sequences (with the exception of scenes where the music is an important part of the *real* background, e.g. lovers in a dance-hall) but should be reserved for stylised pieces of writing as when a narrator is speaking in verse or a character thinking aloud (like a factory worker soliloquising to the rhythm of a machine or a traveller to the rhythm of a train).

A small minority of radio-dramatic programmes, of which *Christopher Columbus* is one, were conceived from the start as joint literary and musical works. In such cases the above remarks still apply. The music, though much more conspicuous, must still be strictly functional, subordinated to the dramatic purpose of the whole; the music must not attempt to usurp the primary role and turn the whole thing into a concert.

(xii)
Conclusion

Most of the above generalisations are elementary, although many radio-dramatic works, including my own, often fail to conform to them. I have been expressing what I consider the norms of this kind of writing, but I should now add the warning that here, as in any other medium, it is fatal to let yourself be victimised by 'the rules'. G. K. Chesterton said that, if a thing is worth doing at all, it is worth doing badly. A similar paradox is true of any artistic medium: if its rules are worth keeping, they are also—on occasion—worth breaking. I trust therefore that this Introduction will not be regarded as an *ex cathedra* lecture. In any art-form a practitioner must be an empiricist. Any generalisations which he makes should be proved or refuted in practice. The medium is there for anyone who wants to degeneralise.

For remarks on *Christopher Columbus* I refer the reader to the Appendix on page 88. I would here make acknowledgment to Mr. Dallas Bower who suggested the programme in the first place and later produced it, and to Mr. William Walton whose music supplied a third dimension that this printed text must lack.

L. M.

Addendum (to page 12).—I had overlooked a case where radio scores most heavily, i.e. in *soliloquy*. Try any of Shakespeare's self-communings close to the microphone.

ACT ONE

DOUBT. No, it cannot be done, it cannot be done.
Here on the shore of the final sea
Our windows open on unreality,
The bitter rubric of the sinking sun—
Ne plus ultra. This is the Western edge
Of the established world, the ocean wall
Beyond which none may pass. To pass
Would lead to nothing at all.
DOUBT CHORUS. West of Europe all is dark
Water and uncertainty;
Never seaman dare embark
On that desert of the sea;
On those waves of nullity
Never venturer may sail—
All who try shall fail, shall fail.
FAITH. Yes, but it *can* be done, it *can* be done.
Wise men have proved the world is round:
Follow the sun to the west and you are bound
To come on unknown lands which know the sun.
Westward! Westward! Legendary isles
Call our ships to sea and who knows where
We shall come to port! We know,
We know there is something *there*.
FAITH CHORUS. West of Europe lies a world
Never heard of, never seen,
But the sails that still are furled
Soon shall reach a new demesne.
All the things that might have been—
When we cross the Western Sea,
All those things shall be, shall be.

A room in Lisbon, 1484.
Three middle-aged Portuguese are having a friendly back-bite.

JOSÉ. Who is this man Columbus?

[21]

ARTUR. Christopher Columbus!
ALFREDO. A madman!
ARTUR. Not a madman, my friend. An impostor.
JOSÉ. What's he doing in Portugal?
    Where does he come from anyway?
ALFREDO. He comes from God knows where.
ARTUR. A very shady customer.
ALFREDO. Think of him going to the King!
ARTUR. Well, the King wouldn't take any nonsense.
ALFREDO. Nonsense isn't the word for it.
    That man's schemes are lunacy.
JOSÉ. Either of you ever seen him?
ALFREDO. I've seen him. He's dangerous.
ARTUR. I've seen him. He's deep.
    Here in Lisbon I saw him one time in a bookshop
    Taking down notes when he thought no one was
      looking.
    His hair's going grey, he's got a hooky nose—
ALFREDO. And a mad look in his eye.
    Time I saw him he couldn't stop talking—
    Went on and on and on about his land in the West.
    Land in the West! You'd have thought
    You were listening to a drunken sailor;
    That's the kind of talk you hear in the taverns on the
      quay.

A guitar creeps in and takes you to a tavern on the quay.
Three rough sailors are swapping stories.

BARTOLOMÉ. I tell you I seen it. With my own eyes I seen it.
FRANCISCO. Go on, Pedro. Have another drink.
BARTOLOMÉ. It was when we was becalmed in Madeira.
    On certain days in Madeira
    You can see high land to the West.
FRANCISCO. Aye, when you've been drinking.
CARLOS. Easy there. I've seen things too. On the island of
    Graciosa—
FRANCISCO. Lay off it, the pair of you.
CARLOS. There was two corpses washed up on to the beach—
    Must have drifted in from the West.

[22]

Wide cheekbones they had and a yellow skin—
BARTOLOMÉ. And you know what *I* seen?
We was sailing off the Azores and we picked up a
piece of wood—
Carved wood it was, with queer figures on it,
Not like aught any of *us* had met with.
FRANCISCO. To hell with all these stories. I suppose
You'll be telling me next you believe in Atlantis
And all them other places—Zipangu and Antilia!
CARLOS. I believe in 'em surely. Why, man, don't you find
'em
Marked on our sheepskin charts?
BARTOLOMÉ. That's right. Antilia and Zipangu....
Aye, and Vineland and Hy Brasil....
And the Isle of the Seven Cities.
CARLOS. And the Fortunate Islands where no one grows old.
BARTOLOMÉ. And the islands of dog-headed men.
And men with only one eye....

The guitar stops and the voices die away.

CARLOS. Hy Brasil....
FRANCISCO. The Fortunate Islands....
BARTOLOMÉ. Zipangu....
CARLOS. Antilia....
FRANCISCO. Atlantis....

The indignant Portuguese continue their indignation.

ALFREDO. The kind of talk you hear from drunken sailors!
What right have these damned foreigners
To think they can come to Lisbon and sell us
something for nothing,
Sell us a midsummer dream of Land in the West
Or a western route to Asia?
I wish the fellows would get out of Portugal.
ARTUR. They say that he's got out already.
To escape arrest, so they say.
JOSÉ. That's good news. Where'll he go to?
ARTUR. Spain presumably. Same old story.
Work away like a mole till he gets a royal
audience—

[23]

In Spain that will take some time—
Then he will go to the King or the Queen or both
And tell them he knows for certain—
Mark what I say: for certain—
That, if they give him a ship, he will sail her West,
Discover islands and mainlands in the Ocean Sea—
ALFREDO. Well, the Spanish Court won't believe *that*.
JOSÉ. Haven't the money if they did.
Far too busy fighting the Moors at Granada.
ALFREDO. If Columbus goes to Spain they'll probably put him
in gaol.
ARTUR. God knows where they will put him. The man has
no place in a modern community.
He has no place and he has no future.
JOSÉ. No future. He has no future at all.
ALFREDO. NO FUTURE AT ALL. . . .

*There is a pause and you hear the chanting of monks. This is
the end of Compline in the monastery of La Rabida. This is
Spain in 1484.*

PEDRO. Father Prior! Father Prior!
PRIOR. What is it, Brother Pedro?
PEDRO. There is a man at the gate. Am I to let him come in?
PRIOR. You know our rules, Brother Pedro:
Admit all strangers who ask for shelter.
PEDRO. Yes, but this man is different.
One ought to be careful these days.
Before I joined the Order of St. Francis
I was, as you know, a soldier;
I know a dangerous man when I see one.
PRIOR. So do I, Brother Pedro;
You forget I have lived many years in the Court.
What kind of a man is this dangerous stranger?
PEDRO. He is in rags and covered with dust.
He looks like a beggar—except for his manner.
He looks very tired—except for his eyes.
PRIOR. Go and admit him at once.
PEDRO. But Father Prior, he may be a thief or a murderer;
Here at La Rabida

[24]

They sneak over here—over the frontier—from
Portugal.
PRIOR. I do not care if he *is* a thief or a murderer.
Our Holy Founder would not have cared either.
Go and admit him at once.
PEDRO. Yes, Father Prior.
PRIOR. And bring him in here.
I like to meet dangerous men.

While Pedro goes to the gate, the monks chant the Salve *in
the background.*

PEDRO. This way please, Señor.
This is the Prior of our monastery, the Reverend
Juan Pérez.
PRIOR. Welcome, my son. Welcome to La Rabida.
Pause.
May I ask you your name?
COLUMBUS. I am a man from Nowhere. They call me
Christopher Columbus.
My trade is the sea; I am a stranger in Spain—
A voice crying in the wilderness.
I knock at the doors of Kings to offer them an
empire;
But—since they refuse it—I beg my bread.
Pedro laughs.
PRIOR. Brother Pedro!
Kindly go to the refectory.
Fetch some food and some wine for Señor
Columbus.
PEDRO. Yes, Father Prior.
Pedro goes out.
PRIOR. Now, my son, if you will sit here....
You are tired? You have come a long way?
COLUMBUS. I have come a long way ... It is only the beginning.
PRIOR. You say your trade is the sea? Where did you learn
it?
COLUMBUS. At the age of ten in Genoa.
I come of a family of wool-weavers and tapsters
But God gave me a feeling for ships.

[25]

PRIOR. So you are a native of Genoa?

COLUMBUS. I am a native of the Kingdom of God.

PRIOR. Here in La Rabida we know about ships;
We are only a couple of miles from the port of
Palos—

COLUMBUS. Palos? That looks west.

PRIOR. Yes, they sail from there down the coast of Africa.

Pedro returns.

PEDRO. Father Prior, here is the food and wine.

COLUMBUS. I am not hungry, Father Prior.

PRIOR. But surely—When did you last eat?

COLUMBUS. This morning, I think. Or maybe yesterday.
But I have no hunger for bread or meat.
Only a hunger to talk.

PRIOR. That can be easily satisfied.
Brother Pedro, go to Brother Antonio.
Tell him we have a guest who shares his interests,
Ask him to join us.

PEDRO. Yes, Father Prior.

Pedro goes out.

PRIOR. Antonio de Marchena—You will like him,
He knows about astrology and cosmography.
And, Brother Pedro, tell him to bring his charts—
His charts and the Mappa Mundi.

PEDRO. Yes, Father Prior.

COLUMBUS. Charts? The charts are all wrong.
Except maybe Toscanelli's—

PRIOR. Who did you say?

COLUMBUS. No matter. It was a map
I saw in Lisbon but I knew it before;
I knew it all in my blood.

Pedro returns with Antonio.

PEDRO. Here is Brother Antonio.

PRIOR. Come in, Brother Antonio.
This is our guest, Señor Christopher Columbus.

ANTONIO. I am happy to meet you, Señor.

COLUMBUS. You are a cosmographer?

ANTONIO. It is my amusement.

COLUMBUS. You know that the world is round?

ANTONIO. There are learned men—eccentrics—who don't
admit it.

COLUMBUS. But *you* admit it?

ANTONIO. Certainly.

COLUMBUS. Good. Then listen to me.

PEDRO (*aside*) The man will be talking all night.

PRIOR. Brother Pedro,
It is time you returned to your duties.

PEDRO. Yes, Father Prior.

Pedro goes out for good.

COLUMBUS. Right. The world is round. That is Point One.
Point Two, Brother Antonio, is this:
You know that in order to reach Asia
People till now have gone to the East?

PRIOR. How else would they go, my son?

COLUMBUS. They would turn their backs on Europe and sail to
the west.
And, if the world is round, that would bring them to
Asia.

ANTONIO. That may be so. No one would dare to try it,
And sail beneath the earth—

COLUMBUS. *I* would dare.

ANTONIO. Has it occurred to you, Señor,
That, if you *did* sail out to the west,
There might be other lands between here and Asia?

COLUMBUS. Yes, there is Zipangu.

PRIOR. Zipangu! A story of Marco Polo's.

ANTONIO. I myself, Father Prior, believe Marco Polo.
I know he did not visit Zipangu himself
But his evidence for it is good.
He says there are many islands in the sea to the east
of Asia.
Seven thousand islands.

COLUMBUS. Seven thousand, four hundred and forty.

PRIOR. Seven thousand islands that have never heard of
Christ.

COLUMBUS. They will hear of Him soon.

PRIOR. Why do you think so?

COLUMBUS. My name is Christopher—that is the Bearer of
Christ.
My name is Columbus—that is the Dove.
You remember the dove of Noah?
It flew across the waters bearing a branch of olive.

[27]

PRIOR. So you want to carry Christ to the Unknown
World?

COLUMBUS. That is my mission.

PRIOR. You cannot do that alone.
You will need material things, you will need
official support.
And I fear you will meet with a refusal.

COLUMBUS. I have met with refusals already.
I have been refused by Kings.

PRIOR. What Kings, my son?

COLUMBUS. Portugal. Portugal refused me.

PRIOR. So now you are trying Spain?

COLUMBUS. Spain ... England ... France.... Anyone who will
have me.

ANTONIO. Spain, I fear, will be the same as Portugal.
They will refuse you too.

PRIOR. That is not certain, Brother Antonio.
Our Queen Isabella has faith.

ANTONIO. Yes, she has faith, but her treasury is empty.
Besides, our King, Ferdinand ...
He likes to be sure of his returns.

PRIOR. Speak softly, Brother Antonio....
Yes, Señor, it is true. The State Treasuries are empty.
The war with the Moors is still going on—
God knows when it will end.
Aragon and Castile are drained of money and
blood;
Our first business is to take Granada,
To purge our land of the Sign of the Crescent.
And we cannot run after the moon while the earth is
in chaos.
You are impatient, my son, to find new worlds,
But before we do that, we must put the old in order.

COLUMBUS. My new world, Father Prior, might help the old.

PRIOR. My son, you are younger than I am.
You must forgive me if in my old age
My vision is narrower than yours.
All I can see is Europe and that is enough—
Quarrels within the state and quarrels without
And, above all, the threat of the false gods.
It is only thirty years since Constantinople,

The second pillar of Christendom, fell to the Infidel.
You would not remember that personally.
COLUMBUS. I remember all things personally.
All that has happened to man since the fall of Adam.
PRIOR. And you know why Adam fell?
Because he had eaten the fruit of the Tree of
Knowledge—
The forbidden tree that gives men fancies,
That makes them cry for the moon.
You yourself, my son—
The taste of that fruit is strong in your mouth.
ANTONIO. Father Prior!
PRIOR. What is it, Brother Antonio? I thought you were
falling asleep.
ANTONIO. I've never been less asleep in my life.
It is this map. There!
Antonio tears up his chart.
PRIOR. What are you doing? Why have you torn it up?
ANTONIO. Because it is wrong. It is a lie.
PRIOR. It's your own map. Didn't you make it yourself?
ANTONIO. I made it myself and it's wrong.
This man has proved it is wrong.
Señor Columbus, I thank you.
My map ended on the shore of Europe
But you have shown me the truth.
The shore of Europe was the end of the world
But from this day on the world is endless.
I shall make a new map tomorrow.
PRIOR. Señor Columbus,
You seem to have made an impression on Brother
Antonio;
That is something unusual.
Brother Antonio,
Do you really believe that Señor Columbus—
Or anyone else for that matter—
Could sail out west from Europe and come to land?
ANTONIO. I would not have believed it before tonight. . . .
But now I do, Father Prior, now I do.
PRIOR. In that case we must see what can be done.
Señor Columbus,
You do not know it but I have the ear of the Queen,

For many years I was her Father Confessor—
COLUMBUS. Then you will send me to the Queen?
PRIOR. Not so fast, my son. Their Catholic Majesties
Are not so easy to approach.
The Queen's Confessor now is Hernando de
Talavera.
I will give you an introduction to Talavera.
ANTONIO. And there he had better be careful.
PRIOR. That is true. I must warn you.
Talavera is a holy man but he is not like myself
Or Brother Antonio here.
You, my son, have a strange manner of speaking,
So be careful when you meet Talavera;
Pride is something he hates.
You must approach him with proper humility,
Explain your scheme to him in moderate language—
COLUMBUS. I will tell Talavera the truth.
That is all he can ask for.
ANTONIO. Perhaps it is more than he asks for.
PRIOR. Yes, my son. Talavera,
He has no interest in knowledge for itself,
He has no interest in worldly glory.
He is a servant of God.
He may very possibly think your scheme is mad
And, what is worse, he may think it sacrilegious.
COLUMBUS. That is all right. I will quote him the Bible.
Where can I find him?
PRIOR. He is at the moment in Cordoba.
I will send you there in a few days' time.
It is a short journey.
ANTONIO. I would call it a long one.

DOUBT. Finding his way by starts and gleams,
Plotting imponderable schemes,
A haggard pilgrim drunk with dreams
He plods the dusty land of Spain
To call upon the indifferent Court,
On priests and nobles for support,
But he will call in vain, in vain.
DOUBT CHORUS. Endeavour as it can

The over-eager soul
Shall never reach its goal—
The truth denied to man.

FAITH. The man the populace despise—
There is a flame that never dies
Upon the altars of his eyes;
He will not break, he will not bend,
His hands are tied by Church and State,
He runs the gauntlet of the great
But he shall conquer in the end.

FAITH CHORUS. His inner eye is true,
He knows that he is free
To see what none can see,
What none can do, to do.

COLUMBUS. Now the game is beginning; now I am on the move.
Whether they want to or not, they will have to
listen.
I am Christopher, the Bearer of Christ,
I am the Dove that travels the world,
And the words that I speak are the words that I hear
And the words that I hear are the words of God.
I am the last Apostle. Let them give me a ship
And I will carry Christ to the world that no one
knows,
I will remake the maps and I will remake
The destinies of the human race. Give me a ship
And I will pass the gates of the West and build
A bridge across the Future. Look out there—
All you see is a waste of waters, the heaving
Bosom of the indifferent childless sea,
The drunken marble of the toppling wave,
The edge of the horizon or the explosive
Filigree of spindrift—That is all you see
But I see so much more.
In my hand I hold the key of the West,
I have come to Spain with that key in my hand,
I shall open my hand to the powers of Spain
And say: 'Do you see this?
This is the key to glory, the key to a new world.

Will you allow me to use it?'
That is what I shall say to the powers of Spain
And, whether they want to or not, they will have to
listen.

Fanfare.

HERALD. Fray Hernando de Talavera, Monte Jerónimo,
Confessor to Her Catholic Majesty; Bishop of Avila!
The Lord Bishop is granting an audience
To an unknown person, one Christopher Columbus.
Pause
TALAVERA. Señor Columbus
I cannot really think that you are serious;
You come to me here out of nowhere,
A foreigner with no credentials,
And you ask me to procure you an audience
With her Catholic Majesty herself.
Her Majesty, Queen Isabella of Spain,
Is busy with the war with the Moors;
She has other things to think of
Than a wild goose chase after something that does
not exist.
You have not, Señor, given me a single ground
To think your proposals feasible. I admit
You have quoted the Holy Scriptures to me;
perhaps
I ought to remind you of the saying
That the devil can quote scripture to his purpose.
Your language, Señor, has been immoderate.
However,
I cannot recommend you to the Queen, but seeing
That you are adrift in Spain, I will give you
A letter to one of the grandees of Andalusia,
The Duke of Medina-Sidonia. . . .
Fanfare.
HERALD. The Most Excellent Señor Don Enrique de Guzmán,
Duke of Medina-Sidonia,
Count of Niebla and Señor of Sanlúcar de
Barrameda.

MEDINA-SIDONIA.

    Señor Columbus,
    I have listened to your project with the utmost
       attention;
    It has, I may say, the charm of novelty
    At the same time it takes me back to my youth;
    I remember when I had dreams like that myself...
    However, Señor, I am a busy man,
    Running my own estates takes me all my time—
    If you want someone who likes adventure
    And might have more time to discuss this matter,
    I will give you a letter to my peer, the Duke of
      Medina Celi,
    Whose exploits you will have heard of against the
      Moors.

               Fanfare.

HERALD. The most Excellent Señor Don Luís de la Cerda,
    Duke of Medina Celi,
    (Count of Puerto de Santa Maria),
    Señor of Cogolludo, of Gibraleón,
    Of Bembibre, Castrobalcón and of la Peña de
      Valdeña.

MEDINA CELI.

    Señor Columbus
    I am a man of action. What you have told me
    Sounds like a fairy story but it stirs my blood.
    If it were not for this war with the Moors
    I would be half inclined ... But, apart from that,
    Even a Spanish grandee could not espouse your
      cause
    Without the royal authority.
    I know that you want to go direct to the Queen
    But that is quite impossible. For myself,
    I shall be pleased to offer you hospitality.
    Stay in my household as long as you wish. If you
      will only be patient,
    I will, in due time, when circumstances permit,
    Give you a letter to the man who, after Their
      Majesties themselves,
    Is the greatest power in Aragon or Castile—
    I mean Mendoza himself,

[33]

The Grand Cardinal of Spain.
Fanfare.

HERALD. His Eminency the Cardinal,
Don Pedro Gonzalez de Mendoza,
Archbishop of Seville!

MENDOZA. Now, Señor Columbus,
You have come to me from the Duke of Medina
Celi,
In whose household you have stayed two years;
You were sent to him by the Duke of Medina
Sidonia
To whom you were sent by Hernando de Talavera
To whom you were sent by the Prior of La Rabida.
Where is all this leading you?

COLUMBUS. I hope, my Lord, to the Queen.

MENDOZA. You have a sanguine temperament.
I have here a letter about you from the Queen's
Confessor,
The most reverend Hernando de Talavera.
You have not seen him, I take it, for two years.

COLUMBUS. He writes to support my cause?

MENDOZA. He writes to tell me you are mad.
Pause.
Talavera is the Queen's Confessor,
She pays great attention to all that he says.
It is a pity you have set him against you.

COLUMBUS. Very well. If Spain will not have me,
I will go to France or England.

MENDOZA. A moment, Señor. Talavera is powerful.
So am I, Señor Columbus.
I will arrange you an audience with the Queen.

The Court of Castile.
Two lackeys.

1ST LACKEY. Who is that fellow sitting in the ante-room?

2ND LACKEY. Sitting? He's been walking up and down,
Up and down the carpet like a caged tiger.
He's waiting to see the Queen.

1ST LACKEY. See the Queen! Who is he?

[34]

He looks no better than us.
2ND LACKEY. He's one of those mad foreigners,
 You ought to have heard how he spoke to me—
 Looked right through me as if I was a sieve.
 I only hope Her Majesty keeps him waiting.
1ST LACKEY. He'll be kept waiting all right.
 She's busy with the Marquesa.
2ND LACKEY. Marquesa de Moya?
1ST LACKEY. Who else? She's the only woman she trusts.

The Queen's Room.

MARQUESA. Your Majesty?
ISABELLA. What is it now, my friend?
MARQUESA. May I not stay for this interview?
ISABELLA. I have told you once. You may not.
MARQUESA. But this man Columbus—
 My husband has been talking to Diego de Deza
 And Deza had been talking to the Cardinal of
 Spain—
ISABELLA. You all of you talk too much.
MARQUESA. But this man Columbus seems a phenomenon.
ISABELLA. My Father Confessor tells me he's a menace.
MARQUESA. Diego de Deza, so my husband says,
 Thinks that his scheme is possible.
 If that is so and if you would further it,
 Think what you would be doing for Spain.
ISABELLA. I hope God will forgive me if I say
 I have done certain things for Spain already;
 Put down faction and cleaned out heresy,
 Reunited the country,
 Restored our old universities,
 Revived the arts and humanities.
 If I can only also defeat the Moors
 I shall not feel ashamed.
MARQUESA. No, Your Majesty, but—
ISABELLA. But what?
MARQUESA. But look at Portugal.
 Look how the Portuguese explored the coasts of
 Africa

[35]

And took it all for themselves.
Why shouldn't *we* do something like that?
ISABELLA. Africa, my dear friend, happened to exist.
If you sail along a coast you can be sure
That you will discover something.
What Señor Columbus asks is a very different
matter.
MARQUESA. But it is much more exciting.
ISABELLA. We do not make our decisions on grounds of
excitement.
My friend, I shall see this man now.
I must ask you to go next door;
Go and practise your instrument.

The Marquesa goes next door and practises her instrument.

MARQUESA (*sings*) 'Down in the Kingdom of Granada
Our soldiers are fighting the Moors,
Our soldiers are all at the wars
Under the Sierra Nevada.'
What can they be talking about so long?
'The snow remains on the peaks
The night is ebony and silver,
And death is a dark river,
Down in the Kingdom of Granada?'
I wonder what this man Columbus is like,
They are having a marathon interview
The evening sun is crawling over the floor . . .
'The scimitars of the Moors
Flash on the towers of the Alhambra;
The cross of Our Lord Christ
Is broken on the Alcazaba.
Orange groves and olive,
Orange blossom and mimosa,
Grow in the shadow of Death
Under the Sierra Nevada.'
What can he be like? Perhaps if I just creep over. . .
Perhaps if I listen at the door . . .
Very dishonourable of me . . .
Faint murmuring of Isabella's voice; then of Columbus.

[36]

That is Columbus now ...
Perhaps if I open it, just the tiniest chink ...
I *must* just see what he's like ...

COLUMBUS (*from the next room*).
Your Majesty,
I must beg leave to correct you.

MARQUESA. God preserve us!

COLUMBUS. You used the word possibility.
What I am proposing is a certainty.

MARQUESA. God in his mercy protect us!
So that is Christopher Columbus!
The man who corrects Isabella.

MARQUESA (*sings*) 'Down in the Kingdom of Granada
The cavaliers and the Hidalgos
Are driving the cattle of the Moors,
Are driving the cavalgada;
The rocks are stained with blood,
Our bones are cold and silver,
For Death is a dark river,
Under the Sierra Nevada.'

The Marquesa's singing recedes as we move next door.

ISABELLA. Señor Columbus,
We Isabella, Queen of Castile and Aragon,
Have listened to all you say,
And we would suggest to you, Señor,
A greater discretion of speech.
It is not the custom in Spain to contradict the
Throne;
But, for this one time, we will pass that over.
Now, Señor, we will speak to you openly.
Our Father Confessor told us you were mad
But your words have stirred our fancy.
You ask us to give you a ship
And to authorise you to sail to the end of the world;
You ask us to send you out into an ocean of
guess-work.

COLUMBUS. Give me a ship and you need not guess any more.
Only give me a ship.

ISABELLA. Matters like this, Señor, are not decided in a word.
  We shall have to consult our partner on the Throne
  Who is at this moment attacking Granada.
  Apart from that we shall have to consult the
      authorities.
COLUMBUS. Who are *they*, Your Majesty?
ISABELLA. Señor, we ask you again to remember to whom you
      are speaking;
  We are not accustomed to be interrupted and
      questioned.
  By the authorities we mean an assemblage of learned
      men,
  With knowledge of the world and of books,
  With knowledge of the soul and of God.
  What you propose may be factually impossible,
  It may also be morally wrong.
  These two points must be decided.
  I will refer them to a Royal Commission
  Consisting of wise men and fathers of the Church;
  They shall decide whether you are right,
  They shall decide whether there is land in the West.
COLUMBUS. But how can they know?
  How can they know I am wrong until I have proved
      myself right?
  How can they know what there is in the West
  While the West is still uncharted?
  Here am I. Give me a ship,
  Let me go to the West and then let them prove me
      wrong.
ISABELLA. We did not say they will prove you wrong—
  We hope ourselves they will not—
  But we will not undertake this thing without their
      authority.
COLUMBUS. Authority! Authority! Authority!
  What authority had Moses to go out into the desert?
ISABELLA. He had the authority of God.
COLUMBUS. Yes, Your Majesty, but I dare swear
  He did not have to wait for the learned men
  To niggle over their books and mumble into their
      beards
  Before he set out on the path that he knew was his.

[38]

ISABELLA. Señor, you forget yourself.
    We, Isabella, Queen of Castile and Aragon,
    Have told you what we will do.
    We will call a Royal Commission.
    That is all, Señor.
    Now you will leave our presence.
    In the other room the Marquesa is still singing.
MARQUESA (*sings*) 'The fountains of the Alhambra
    Are playing upon the marble;
    The hungry eagle hovers
    On the hill of the Alcazaba.'
ISABELLA. (*entering*) Marquesa!
MARQUESA. Your Majesty.
ISABELLA. You may stop making music now.
    Your Señor Columbus has gone.
MARQUESA. Oh he was wonderful.
ISABELLA. How do you know he was wonderful?
    The ladies of my Court do not listen at doors.
MARQUESA. I am sorry, Your Majesty.
    I only listened for a minute.
    Are you going to give him your support?
ISABELLA. I am appointing a Royal Commission.
    I shall make Talavera its president.
MARQUESA. Talavera! But he hates him.
ISABELLA. Talavera is impartial.
    The Commission will meet in Salamanca
    In the Monastery of St. Stephen.

*There is a pause and you hear The Commissioners singing the
Veni Creator; this is drowned in the murmuring of a crowd.*

TALAVERA. Silence in the Court of the Commission!
    The murmuring dies down.
    Fathers of the Church, Doctors of the Law and
        Masters of Letters,
    As President of this Commission
    Appointed by Her Catholic Majesty Queen Isabella
    To investigate the case of Christopher Columbus,
    I here and now after three days' session on this subject,
    Consider that the time has come to make our decision.

If anyone here present wants any further discussion—

1ST VOICE. No, we don't!

2ND VOICE. We've heard enough already.

3RD VOICE. Enough and more than enough.

TALAVERA. Order in the Court!
Does anyone here present want any further
discussion?

DIEGO DE DEZA.
I do, my Lord President.
Murmuring.

TALAVERA. It seems our learned Brother Diego de Deza
Wants some more discussion.

1ST VOICE. No! No! No! No more discussion!

TALAVERA. What are your grounds, Señor, for holding up our
verdict?

DIEGO DE DEZA.
My grounds, my Lord President, are these.
We have now been in session three days
Debating the proposals of Christopher Columbus.
Three days, one would have thought were enough—

2ND VOICE. They *are* enough!

3RD VOICE. Enough and more than enough!

DIEGO DE DEZA.
They would have been had you had open minds
And kept to the point in debate—
But you have done no such thing.

CHORUS. Shame! Shame!

1ST VOICE. Sit down, Señor, sit down.

DIEGO DE DEZA.
I regret very much, my Lord President,
In such a distinguished gathering
To have to lodge a complaint of emotional
prejudice—

1ST VOICE. Sit down, can't you?

DIEGO DE DEZA.
The applicant to our Commission,
Señor Christopher Columbus—
Murmuring.
Has come before us with a perfectly serious
proposal—

2ND VOICE. Perfectly serious!

Laughter.

DIEGO DE DEZA.
> This proposal merits our gravest consideration
> And that for a number of reasons—

3RD VOICE. Tell us *one*!

DIEGO DE DEZA.
> One reason, my brother, is this:
> That, if what Señor Columbus says be true—

VOICES. True! It's *not* true! How could it be true?

TALAVERA. Order in the Court!
> Let our Fellow Commissioner proceed.

DIEGO DE DEZA.
> If what he says be true then we should give him our
> aid
> Because, if his project succeeds—

2ND VOICE. Away with all these ifs.
> If he fails he will make us a laughing stock.

DIEGO DE DEZA.
> Why take failure for granted?
> And why be afraid of laughter?
> The thing after all is possible.
> We admit that the world is a sphere—

3RD VOICE. No, we don't. We don't admit any such thing.

DIEGO DE DEZA.
> I appeal to you, my Lord President.
> I thought it had been agreed that the world is a
> sphere.

TALAVERA. No, Señor, the question whether the world is a
> sphere
> Is still, it would seem, open to dispute.
> In the present discussion, however, this question is
> irrelevant.

DIEGO DE DEZA.
> I beg your pardon, my Lord, but it is not in the
> least irrelevant.
> *If* the world is a sphere—

TALAVERA. Brother Diego de Deza,
> We cannot hold up these proceedings for one
> dissentient.
> I therefore propose without any further ado,
> Seeing that no one has anything further to say—

COLUMBUS. *I* have something to say.

TALAVERA. You have said your piece, Señor Columbus.
　　　　　Further remarks from you would be out of order.
　　　　　　　　　Pause.
　　　　　Gentlemen of the Commission,
　　　　　The question before you is twofold.
　　　　　Señor Columbus has come before this Court
　　　　　To expound a certain theory
　　　　　And make a certain proposal;
　　　　　We have to decide whether his theory is true
　　　　　And, if it is true, whether his proposal is practical.
　　　　　Previous to your decision,
　　　　　I propose to summarise the evidence—

1ST VOICE. Is that necessary, my Lord President?

TALAVERA. It may not be necessary, Señor.
　　　　　It is the custom.
　　　　　　　　　Pause.
　　　　　Señor Christopher Columbus,
　　　　　Will you oblige me by standing on the rostrum?

4TH VOICE (*aside*).
　　　　　The man's all a-quiver.

5TH VOICE (*aside*).
　　　　　He knows what's coming.

TALAVERA. Thank you, Señor.
　　　　　Christopher Columbus, citizen of Genoa—

COLUMBUS. I am *not* a citizen of Genoa.

TALAVERA. You are not a citizen of Spain
　　　　　You are not a citizen of Portugal;
　　　　　A man must have some country—

COLUMBUS. My country, my Lord, is the Future.
　　　　　　　　Pause: laughter and catcalls.

3RD VOICE. Then what are you doing here?
　　　　　　　　More laughter.

TALAVERA. Order in the Court!
　　　　　I would remind the Commissioners of their dignity.
　　　　　　　　　Pause.
　　　　　Christopher Columbus, you have told us your
　　　　　　theory;
　　　　　And you have explained to us your project.
　　　　　In my opinion—but I do not know
　　　　　Whether the Commission will agree with me—

[42]

5TH VOICE (*aside*).
　　He doesn't know!
4TH VOICE (*aside*)
　　Oh no!
TALAVERA. In my opinion your theory is downright false—
CHORUS. Hear! Hear!... Hear! Hear!...
TALAVERA. Your theory is contrary to common sense—
CHORUS. Hear! Hear!
TALAVERA. Your theory is contrary to Reason—
CHORUS. Hear! Hear!... Hear! Hear!
TALAVERA. Your theory is contrary to Holy Writ
　　And the accepted doctrines of the Church.
CHORUS. Hear! Hear!... *Hear! Hear!*... HEAR! HEAR!
　　　　Pause.
TALAVERA. Many Commissioners have made that point;
　　They have quoted the Scriptures to disprove you,
　　They have quoted the Christian Fathers,
　　They have quoted St. Lactantius and St. Augustine,
　　They have quoted the Law and the Prophets.
COLUMBUS. Prophets!
　　What do they know about prophets?
　　What do you, my Lord President, know about
　　　　prophets?
TALAVERA. Silence, Señor!
COLUMBUS. Have I not quoted you back the prophet Isaiah?
　　Have I not quoted you back the prophet Esdras?
　　Have I not told you the words that I hear myself in
　　　　the night—
　　The still small voice of Almighty God Himself?
　　Uproar; cries of 'Shame!', 'Blasphemy!'
TALAVERA. Señor Columbus! I call you to order!
　　What you have just said is not only contempt of
　　　　court,
　　What you have said is blasphemy.
2ND VOICE. That's right. Blasphemy.
1ST VOICE. Give him to the Inquisition.
CHORUS. Down with Columbus! Down with Columbus!
　　Down with Columbus!
TALAVERA. Order in the Court!
　　Christopher Columbus,
　　What you have just said precludes further debate.

[43]

You have stood here before this Royal Commission
Consisting of learned men and dignitaries of the
  Church,
You have stood here and thrown God in our teeth.
This being so, Señor,
My patience is now at an end—
COLUMBUS. And so is mine, my Lord.
You and your Royal Commission—
For three days you have baulked the issue,
Three days of prevarication and obscuration,
Three days of the closed mind and the lying
  tongue—
CHORUS. Shame! Shame! Shame!
COLUMBUS (*against uproar*).
I have heard the opinions of your learned body;
They are like so many dead leaves
Blown hither and thither in an endless maze
Of ancient ignorance and prejudice—
A labyrinth of lies.
                    Uproar.
TALAVERA. Order in the Court!
My fellow Commissioners,
I am not surprised this time at your loss of control.
This man has convicted himself out of his own
  mouth
As either a wilful heretic or a madman.
There is no need for me to conclude my summary.
This man has asked us for our official approval.
There is only one answer to give.
CHORUS (*mounting*).
No! No! No!
No! No! No!

The repeated negatives mount into a musical chorus.

DOUBT CHORUS. No ... No ... No ...
            Never again!
            His hope was thrown away
            And all his work in vain.
DOUBT. Broken the golden bowl

[44]

And gone the morning dream,
No one can now redeem
The desolated soul.
Alone he toils along
A never-ending street
Where all his hopes are wrong
And all his life defeat.

DOUBT CHORUS. Defeat! Defeat! Defeat!
                          Defeat! Defeat!
                          He knows his hopes are wrong
                          And all his life defeat.

*There is a pause as several years elapse. A guitar emerging
from tipsy chatter takes us to a humble tavern.*

MANUEL. Wine there! Wine!
TAPSTRESS. Not so fast, fellow. How many hands have I got?
                   You've both had a skinful already. Why can't you
                   behave?
                   Why can't you be decent and quiet like the
                   gentleman over in the corner?
MANUEL. Because we bain't gentlemen.
JUAN. What's that fellow in the corner anyway?
            I seen him before some place.
MANUEL. He looks a bit crazy to me.
TAPSTRESS. He's a man that's come down in the world.
                   He was news one time.
                   Used to be received by the nobility.
JUAN. Fancy that now. Look at his ragged cloak.
MANUEL. Let's go and give him a drink.
TAPSTRESS. Don't you go near him. He's touchy.
JUAN. You can't frighten *us*. What's his name?
TAPSTRESS. Señor Columbus.
JUAN. Hey you, Señor! Señor Columbus!
            We want you to drink with us.
TAPSTRESS. Leave him alone.
IST PEASANT *(loudly)*
                   Maybe he's deaf.
                   Drink, Señor, drink!
                   We want you to drink with us.

COLUMBUS. You want me to drink with you?

JUAN. That's right.

MANUEL. Your health, Señor Columbus.

COLUMBUS. Thank you. Thank you very much.

JUAN. What are you thinking about, Señor?
Remembering something?

COLUMBUS. No, my friend, I'm forgetting something.

Laughter.

JUAN. That's a good one. Forgetting something!
Have another drink if you want to forget,
Have another drink and forget the whole world.

COLUMBUS. And forget the whole world?
It will do if I forget just half of it.

MANUEL. Half of it?

JUAN. He must mean women.

COLUMBUS. No, my friend, I don't mean women.
There is one woman I love but she is easy to forget.

JUAN. They all are. They all are.

COLUMBUS. When you have seen someone then you can forget
them.
But what you have never seen—that's what sticks
in your mind.

MANUEL. I don't tumble to that.

JUAN. Don't understand what you mean.

COLUMBUS. Look at it like this.
You know what it is to be homesick?

MANUEL. I have never been away from my home.

COLUMBUS. That makes no difference.
Maybe you've been homesick for the home you
never had.

MANUEL. That makes no sense neither.

COLUMBUS. Oh yes, it does. Go and look at the sunset
When the sky is a lather of crimson and coral
And the bulging sun, over-ripe with knowledge,
Glides back into the womb of the sea.
Don't you feel as you watch him sink—
Don't you feel an envy of the sun?
It is so easy for him to travel out to the West
And see what none of us have seen.

Pause.

JUAN. You want to be like the sun?

If that's so, you've got no right to be here.
What are you doing sitting here in the corner?
The sun don't sit in no corners.
Always moving the sun is. Always moving.
COLUMBUS. You are quite right, my friend.
Pause.
Yes, you're right.
It's time for me to move on.
MANUEL. Hey! What's the hurry?
JUAN. I didn't mean it serious.
Sit down, Señor. Have another drink.
COLUMBUS. No; you've taught me my lesson. Now I must leave
you.
JUAN. It's too late to travel this time of night.
COLUMBUS. It's never too late to travel.
JUAN. But where in God's name are you going?
COLUMBUS. I'm going out of this country
I'm shaking the dust of Spain from my feet.
I'm going where men will know who I am.
Pause.
But first I must call at Cordoba.
JUAN. Cordoba? I know a woman in Cordoba.
COLUMBUS. So do I. That's why I'm going there.
Beatriz Enríquez. I have to say goodbye to her.
JUAN. So she's expecting you?
COLUMBUS. No, she's not. Why should she be?
I haven't seen her for years.
She does not expect me back.

In Cordoba someone is singing.

BEATRIZ (*sings*). When will he return?
Only to depart.
Harrowed by the omen
Of his restless heart;
Bondsman of the Voice,
Rival of the Sun,
Viceroy of the sunset
Till his task be done.

Though he is my love

He is not for me;
What he loves is over
Loveless miles of sea
Haunted by the West,
Eating out his heart—
When will he return?
Only to depart.

As she stops singing her woman cries from the doorway.

WAITING WOMAN.
Doña Beatriz! Doña Beatriz!

BEATRIZ. What is it, Maria?
Have you seen a ghost?.

WAITING WOMAN.
He has come back, Doña Beatriz.
He is here.

BEATRIZ. Who has come back?

Pause.

You do not mean . . .

WAITING WOMAN.
Yes, Doña Beatriz. Señor Columbus.
He arrived in Cordoba this morning.

BEATRIZ. Where is he now?

WAITING WOMAN.
Here, Doña Beatriz, here. Go to the window.
He is down in the patio sitting on the edge of the
fountain.
Go to the window and see him.
Or shall I tell him to come up?

BEATRIZ. Tell him nothing. . . . Leave me alone.
Get back to your room and stay there.

WAITING WOMAN.
Yes, Doña Beatriz.

The waiting woman goes out.
Beatriz goes to the window and looks down into the patio.

BEATRIZ. Now . . . Softly . . . Softly . . .
No, there is no one in the patio,
I cannot see for the sun
And the leaves and the shadows of leaves, the net of
shadow and dazzle.
Would that be him sitting on the edge of the
fountain?

Or is that a shadow too?
If I shade my eyes with my hand . . .
>   *Pause.*
Yes, it is, it is . . . How grey his hair is.
It is so like him to come and sit in the patio
When he knows I must be here.
Softly, Beatriz, do not cry out;
He must not see you; no,
You must take your cloak and slip away.
What right has he after these years
To come back into my life like a burning ghost
And sit on the edge of my fountain troubling the
>   water with a stick,
Teasing the carp? What right
Has this man who is always passing through,
Passing by and beyond, to turn again
And knock at a door that is overgrown with ivy?
No, I will take my cloak, I will close my lips,
Once and for all I will—
As she is turning from the window Columbus catches sight of her.
COLUMBUS (*from below*).
>   Beatriz!
>   *Pause.*
>   Beatriz! Is that you?
BEATRIZ. Why have you come back?
COLUMBUS. To say goodbye.
BEATRIZ. You said goodbye to me before,
>   When you left me to go to Salamanca,
>   When you left me to go before the Royal
>   Commission—
COLUMBUS. Don't mention that;
>   All that is Ancient History.
>   May I come up?
BEATRIZ. No, you had better not. What is the use?
>   When you come on a visit
>   The light is always behind you,
>   The shadow of your departure crosses the door
>   before you;
>   I am too tired, Christopher . . .
>   Where are you going this time?
COLUMBUS. I am on my way out of Spain.

I am looking for a country where men have faith
And where their rulers have vision.
BEATRIZ. No one has more vision—or faith—than Isabella.
COLUMBUS. Don't talk to me about your Queen Isabella.
All you Spaniards have betrayed me.
Your Queen is afraid of her Confessor, Talavera,
Your King thinks only of himself,
Your Court is a circus of knaves and fools,
Of short-sighted bigots and long-fingered thieves.
Pause.
May I come up now?
BEATRIZ. I told you it is no use.
So you are leaving Spain? By land or sea?
COLUMBUS. By sea, from Palos.
I shall call on the way at La Rabida
To say goodbye to Prior Juan Pérez.
Now, Beatriz, since you will not let me come up
I will take this rose from your patio
And I will be on my way.
BEATRIZ. But, Christopher, wait ... Wait!
You have no right to take a rose from my patio.
You have no right to come here at all, but now you
have come,
You cannot leave me like that ...
Yes, you had better come up.

*After another pause you hear the monks again, chanting the
Kyrie Eleison. Columbus is back at La Rabida.*

PRIOR. So, my son, you are leaving Spain?
COLUMBUS. I am leaving Spain for good.
PRIOR. That is a great mistake. Haven't you heard the news?
COLUMBUS. What news, Father Prior?
PRIOR. Granada is about to capitulate.
The war with the Moors is finished.
COLUMBUS. Praised be God for that!
All the same I am leaving this country.
PRIOR. In spite of the Fall of Granada?
COLUMBUS. How can that affect me?
PRIOR. Don't be so foolish, my son.

I know your sojourn in Spain
Has been long and hard and disappointing ...
But now Spain will be different.
The victory over the Moors is a great one,
A new life will come into this people,
There is no telling what they may undertake
That before they would not have dreamt of.
No, my son, do not be stubborn.
Granada is about to surrender:
Take a horse—the best horse that you can—
And ride to Granada at once,
Wait for the Queen when she enters Granada,
Press your suit while the moment is ripe,
Ride to Granada at once, ride to Granada. ...

*After a pause a triumphant chorus is heard. You are now in the
streets of Granada.*

CHORUS (*singing*). Granada has fallen! Granada has fallen!
    The triumph of Spain has atoned for her loss.
    Granada has fallen; the sign of the Crescent
    Has bowed in the end to the sign of the Cross.
    Granada has fallen. Our Queen Isabella
    Has entered Granada with pennons and drums.
    The Old Age was iron; the New Age is golden;
    The Gold Age is coming—oh see where it
        comes!
    Granada has fallen. The long days of torment
    And bloodshed are over; the battle is done
    And we are the victors. Granada has fallen
    And Spain's resurrection today has begun.

OBSERVER. Today ... Today ... Today!
    The most wonderful day in our history.
    From where I stand on the top of this turret
    The whole of this city of Granada is a sea of sound
        and colour—
    Brass and brocade, jewels and banners,
    The plumes of the knights like spray

[51]

When the sun is dancing on the sea.
The Royal Procession is winding through the
  resounding streets,
Ferdinand in silver and gold, Isabella in diamonds,
The sunlight catches in her auburn hair
And her horse's trappings reach to the ground.
Yes, I can see it all but I cannot take it in;
This is the end of our Ten Years' War,
This is the end of the Moorish occupation,
The end of a number of things,
The beginning of many more . . .
The whole town is drunk with drums and trumpets,
The eyes of all the world are fixed upon Granada—
Yes, I can see it all . . . I can see it all . . .

COLUMBUS. And I too—I can see it all:
The cavalcade of those who have won Granada,
Of those who have failed Columbus.
Here I stand, unmarked, among the goggling
  crowd,
In the shimmer of silks and the clamour of bronze,
And I alone have no feeling of triumph.
Or rather I have—but it is not enough;
I must go to the Queen and tell her it is not enough.
I can imagine a greater day than this,
A greater conquest; I see
The banners of Castile and of Christ
Carried in triumph, entering
Nobler gates than the gates of Granada—
I mean the Gates of the West.
I must go to the Queen at once and point across the
  sea
To those invisible gates and open my hand thus
And say 'Your Majesty, here is the key;
Only give me a ship.'

After a pause Columbus repeats himself.
But now Isabella is really there to hear him.

COLUMBUS. Give me a ship, Your Majesty, give me a ship.
Need we delay any longer?

ISABELLA. We shall not delay any longer;
 Your project, Señor Columbus,
 Your proposed voyage of discovery—
 Now that our hands are no longer tied by the
  Moors—
 Excites our warmest interest.
 What we propose is this:
 We shall appoint another Royal Commission—
 What is wrong, Señor?
COLUMBUS. If you appoint another Royal Commission,
 I might as well jump off the top of the Alhambra.
ISABELLA. Control your impatience, Señor.
 This is a great—a momentous—undertaking.
 It has to be begun under the proper auspices.
COLUMBUS. And who, may I ask Your Majesty,
 I ask it with all humility,
 Who is to be the president of this Commission?
ISABELLA. The Commission will be on the same basis as before
 Its President will be the same as before.
COLUMBUS. You mean Talavera? In that case—
ISABELLA. A moment, Señor. It is several years now
 Since you appeared before him. At that time
 Your conduct before the Court was such
 As to excite his displeasure—
COLUMBUS. As to excite his hatred.
ISABELLA. Our Father Confessor does not hate;
 He is a saintly character. However,
 It is true that he can be provoked; therefore, Señor
  Columbus,
 We would remind you to exercise discretion.
 You are going before this Commission
 With our own recommendation;
 All you need do is to be discreet.
 There are certain formalities to be settled,
 And your own status made clear;
 So, whatever you do, make a show of humility,
 Do not offend Talavera again,
 Moderate your demands.

A fanfare introduces the Second Commission.

TALAVERA. Señor Columbus,
As president of this Commission called by royal
demand
To authorise your voyage into the Western Ocean,
It is my duty to tell you that our body
If it is to sanction your undertaking,
Can only give its sanction on certain terms.
COLUMBUS. Thank you, my Lord President. I have terms of my
own.
Murmuring.
TALAVERA. Indeed, Señor? What are they?
COLUMBUS. My Lord President, Members of the Commission,
If I undertake this voyage of discovery,
I demand in return—
TALAVERA. You *demand*, Señor?
Louder murmuring.
COLUMBUS. I demand in return the following things as my
right:
First, the position of Viceroy and Governor-General
Over all islands and continents that I discover—
1ST VOICE. Viceroy and Governor General!
Laughter and murmurs.
COLUMBUS. And further, I demand to be appointed
Admiral of the Western Ocean; and further—
I demand a tenth part of all the treasure—
Pearls, diamonds, silver, spices, gold—
That shall be found in the lands that I discover.
3RD VOICE. Counting his chickens!
2ND VOICE. He's mad!
COLUMBUS. And further, I demand exclusive
Ownership of one eighth part
Of all the lands discovered, and one eighth part ·
Of all the revenues therefrom; and further—
TALAVERA. That is enough, Señor.
COLUMBUS. Further, I tell you;
I demand that all these rights and dignities and titles
Shall be, by Royal charter, made hereditary,
Confirmed to my descendants, from first-born to
first-born.
Pause.
TALAVERA. Is that all, Señor Columbus?

COLUMBUS. That is all, my Lord President.
> *Hostile laughter.*

TALAVERA. Very good, Señor.
I think the Commission will agree with me
That these demands are absurd.
Unless you withdraw them one and all,
We cannot sanction your enterprise.

COLUMBUS. I will not withdraw anything.
Unless I am made Viceroy and Governor-General
Of the lands that I have discovered,
Unless I am made Grand Admiral of the Ocean,
Unless you grant me every title I ask,
I will not sail at all.

1ST VOICE. You won't sail at all!
> *Laughter.*

TALAVERA. I give you your last chance.
Will you withdraw these demands?

COLUMBUS. No. I will not.

TALAVERA. In that case, as President of this Commission,
I refuse you all further support.

CHORUS. Hear! Hear! . . . Hear! Hear! . . . Hear! Hear!

2ND VOICE. That'll be the end of *you*, Señor Columbus.

COLUMBUS. You are wrong, Señor.
Your Royal Commission for the second time has
rejected me.
I shall not trouble you again.

3RD VOICE. Thank God for that!

COLUMBUS. No, my very dear friends,
I shall go over your heads.
You are not the only people who count in Spain.
There *are* some people who believe in me,
I dare say you may have heard of them.
There is Don Andrés de Cabrera, Marquis of Moya,
There is Don Luís de Santangel, Chancellor of the
Treasury,
There is his Eminency the Cardinal—
Don Pedro Gonzalez de Mendoza.
There is also Isabella of Castile.

> *A fanfare takes you back to the Court.*

ISABELLA. Marquesa, what is the news from your husband?

MARQUESA. He has been talking to Luís de Santangel.
Santangel will loan you the money—
If you wish to accept it.

ISABELLA. Of course I wish to accept it.

MARQUESA. His Majesty will not like it.

ISABELLA. Listen, my dear friend.
I am Queen of Castile in my own right;
If I decide to borrow money from my Treasurer
In order to further any particular project—

MARQUESA. So you do want to help Columbus?

ISABELLA. You knew that surely?
That man's ideas have kept me awake in the night.
It is time for him to put them into action.

MARQUESA. But what about Talavera?
He thinks the whole scheme is unholy.

ISABELLA. Even Talavera may be wrong.
Mendoza thinks the opposite.
His Majesty, I know, agrees with Talavera,
Or rather he doesn't think that the scheme is
unholy—
He merely thinks it a waste of time and money.

MARQUESA. But Santangel on the other hand—
He has a head for business—
He thinks that Columbus may bring you in
millions.

ISABELLA. Quite so. Opinion is divided.
What do we do when opinion is divided in our
Court?
We do, my dear Marquesa, what we want to.
Pause.
And Ferdinand will have to agree to it.

Ferdinand agreed to it. A Fanfare introduces the Herald.

HERALD. On this day the thirteenth of April
In the year of Our Lord Fourteen Hundred and
Ninety-two
In the name of the Holy Trinity and Eternal Unity,
We Don Ferdinand and Doña Isabella,

[56]

By the grace of God, King and Queen of Castile,
Leon, Aragon, Sicily, Granada, Toledo, Valencia,
Galacia, Majorca, Seville, Sardinia, Corsica,
Murcia, Jaén, Algarve, Algesiras, Gibraltar and the
    Canary Islands,
Count and Countess of Barcelona,
Lords of Biscay and Molina,
Dukes of Athens and Neopatria,
Counts of Roussillon and Cerdan,
Marquises of Orestan and Goziano,
Have seen a patent of grace signed with our names
    and sealed with our seal,
Drawn up as follows . . .
COLUMBUS. They have given me all that I asked—
Let Talavera laugh it off if he can.
Admiral of the untravelled ocean!
Viceroy of the Unknown World!
They have promised me three ships. I shall sail from
    Palos.

END OF ACT I

ACT TWO

You hear the music and chatter of a port. This is Palos.
Two old longshoremen are gossiping on the quay.

VASCO. What be goin' on in port?
LUÍS. Hast not heard? 'Tis they three ships.
    Fittin' of 'em up for Columbus.
VASCO. Ha! Ha! Ha!
    Martín Pinzón, I hear, be a-goin' too.
LUÍS. Martín Pinzón? 'Tis true.
    I'd have thought he'd have more sense.
    He's a rare good seaman, Martín Pinzón.
VASCO. What can he want, takin' up with Columbus?
LUÍS. God knows what he can want. He has his work cut
    out,
    Tryin' for to sign on crews.
    Nobody wants to sail with 'un.
    You can't blame 'em neither.
    No one in his senses would go on this here trip;
    When they get out West there they'll topple off of
    the world,
    Go right over the edge.
VASCO. So no one will sign on?
LUÍS. Hardly a dozen so far.
    And they three ships be small 'uns.
    The Santa Maria—and she be biggest of three—
    She be two hundred tons or two hundred and
    thirty.
    Nay, man, they'll never raise their crews.
    Not unless they opens the jails.
VASCO. Wouldn't do that, would they?
LUÍS. No knowing what they would do.
    Whole business be crazy.

TOWN CRIER.
    Oyez! Oyez! Oyez!

Hearken to the Royal Proclamation:
We Don Ferdinand and Dona Isabella,
By the grace of God, King and Queen of Castile,
To all magistrates, in our cities and towns,
To all officers of the law and governors of the
        prisons:
Be it known to you that we
Have ordered Christopher Columbus
To proceed to sea for the despatch of certain
Business in our service. And in so much as
He has met with difficulty for this purpose
In the raising the proper crews,
We hereby proclaim an amnesty
To all such persons at present in prison
For the breaking the laws of this realm
As will consent to report at our port of Palos
To man the three ships of the said Christopher
        Columbus.

Now you hear the tramp of the jail-birds.

PINZÓN. Keep in line there. Keep in the line.
        Who comes next?
BARTOLOMÉ. I do, master.
PINZÓN. Where are you from?
BARTOLOMÉ. Prison in Seville.
PINZÓN. What were you in for?
BARTOLOMÉ. Robbery with violence.
PINZÓN. Very good. Sign on at the quay.
        Who comes next?
CARLOS. I do.
PINZÓN. Where are you from?
CARLOS. Prison in Ronda.
PINZÓN. What were you in for?
CARLOS. Coining false money.
PINZÓN. Sign on at the quay. Next!
        Where are you from?
FRANCISCO. Prison in Cabra.
PINZÓN. What were you in for?
FRANCISCO. Murder.

PINZÓN. Right. Sign on at the quay.
It looks as if we shall have a crew after all.

STOREKEEPER: *check these over:*
A third of hard tack, a third of salted flour ...
Wine, bacon, vinegar, oil,
Cheese, peas, beeves, beans,
Stockfish, lentils, honey, raisins,
Hoops, pitch, nails, nets,
Hardware, tallow, oakum ...

*As the storekeeper's inventory fades away, you hear a woman
singing in empty space.*

There be three ships
Down on the quay
Waiting to sail
The Western Sea;
Three lonely ships
Will leave this shore
And we shall see them
Nevermore.

Three ships upon
A hopeless quest
To break the spell
That binds the West,
Three lonely ships
Will leave this shore
And we shall see them
Nevermore.

The voice of Pinzón brings back the world of business.

PINZÓN. Señor Columbus.
COLUMBUS. What is it, Señor Pinzón?
PINZÓN. All three ships are ready and seaworthy.
Laden and manned and ready to sail.

COLUMBUS. In that case, Señor Pinzón ...
In that case we sail tomorrow.
PINZÓN. Very good, Señor. Tomorrow.
SERVANT (*entering*).
Señor Columbus! Señor Columbus!
COLUMBUS. Why do you come in my presence without
knocking?
SERVANT. I am sorry, Señor. There is a lady outside.
COLUMBUS. Ask her to come in.
PINZÓN. I will leave you then.
COLUMBUS. I will see you tomorrow, Señor Pinzón.
Remember to check that matter of the biscuits.
PINZÓN. One pound of biscuits per man per day,
Two litres of wine per man per day,
Two thirds of a pound—But it's not so easy;
How can we possibly know how many days—
COLUMBUS. That, Señor, is irrelevant.
PINZÓN. Very good, Señor. Hasta la vista.
COLUMBUS. Hasta la vista.
The servant re-enters.
SERVANT. Doña Beatriz Enríquez.
COLUMBUS. Leave me.
Pause.
Beatriz ...
BEATRIZ. I heard you were due to sail.
I came on horseback from Cordoba.
COLUMBUS. That was a mistake, Beatriz.
BEATRIZ. I wouldn't have come but I had something to tell you.
COLUMBUS. You cannot have anything new to tell me.
BEATRIZ. Yes, I have. Something entirely new.
Or perhaps I should say it is something very old—
Old for the race of women but new for me.
COLUMBUS. If you want me back, Beatriz—
BEATRIZ. I do not want you back, Señor.
I know you are going away for ever—
But then you've always been away.
When you and I were together in a locked room
You still were further away than the furthest planet.
COLUMBUS. If you know that, why've you come here now?
BEATRIZ. Because I have something to tell you.
COLUMBUS. Then for God's sake tell me. I have no time to spare.

BEATRIZ. No ... I cannot tell you. You have no imagination.
COLUMBUS. *I* have no imagination!
BEATRIZ. When are you sailing?
COLUMBUS. Tomorrow. Early in the morning.
BEATRIZ. Then perhaps tonight ...
COLUMBUS. Tonight I shall go to the monastery of La Rabida
And spend the night on my knees.
BEATRIZ. You have good reason.
                    Pause.
        Goodbye.
COLUMBUS. Beatriz ...
BEATRIZ. If you are praying the whole night
You might say a prayer for me.
Goodbye, Christopher, goodbye ...

*Beatriz vanishes and morning succeeds her. A crowd has come
to the quay to see Columbus off. The gulls are crying and the
two old longshoremen are waiting for something sensational.*

VASCO. A fine morning, Luís.
LUÍS. Aye, 'tis a fine morning.
You be up early.
VASCO. I want to be in at the death.
LUÍS. So do whole town seemingly.
Never seen such a crowd here.
VASCO. Where be old madman himself?
'Captain Christopher Columbus'?
LUÍS. On his way down from La Rabida
They say as he spent the night a-praying.
VASCO. Reckon he had good need to.
And all them other poor devils.
LUÍS. *They* spent night in pot-houses.
VASCO. 'Let us eat and drink for tomorrow us die.'
Lord have mercy on all of 'em.
                Now we hear the drumming.
LUÍS. That'll be 'un now. Look 'ee yonder.
Yon be banner of Castile—the gold castle on the red
ground.
VASCO. Aye, and yon be friars of St. Francis—
See their brown hoods in crowd.
Who be they two fellows in front?

[62]

One of 'em walking with great big strides
And the tall one a-going along as if he was floating.
LUÍS. The tall one look like old Juan Pérez—
He be prior of La Rabida.
One that's striding must be Columbus himself.
VASCO. Be that Columbus himself?
Ha! Ha! Ha! What's all the hurry?
The crowd swells up and the drums come nearer.
VASCO. What be old Prior up to?
He bain't sailing, surely?
LUÍS (*shouting*)
What did 'ee say? Can't hear.
VASCO (*shouting*).
Prior? *He* bain't sailing?
LUÍS. Prior of La Rabida? Nay.
He be come to bless the ships.
There is dead silence for the Blessing.
PRIOR. O God, Lord of the Heaven and Earth and of the
wide sea, we humbly pray Thee out of Thy infinite
mercy to bless and hallow these three ships, sailing
today from this port of Palos to a bourne which no
man knows.
Per Dominum.
CHORUS. Per Dominum.
*The crowd begins to chant the Litany of the Saints. Columbus
is heard crying with full voice over it.*
COLUMBUS. In the name of the Holy Trinity—
Weigh the anchor.
VOICE. Aye, aye, Captain. Anchor up.
MATE. Hands to the capstan. Break her out.
The Litany continues but is drowned in a Capstan Shanty.
SOLO. We're bound upon a wild goose quest—
pero yo ya no soy yo—
SOLO. To find an empire in the West—
ni mi casa es ya mi casa.

SOLO. Goodbye to Spain and the Spanish shore—
CHORUS. pero yo ya no soy yo—
SOLO. For *we* won't see our wives no more—
CHORUS. ni mi casa es ya mi casa.

SOLO. The life on shore was not so bad—

E
[63]

CHORUS.   pero yo ya no soy yo—
SOLO.   And now we're here we know we're mad—
CHORUS.   ni mi casa es ya mi casa.

SOLO.   So goodbye father and mother mine—
CHORUS.   pero yo ya no soy yo—
SOLO.   You can drink my health in muscadine—
CHORUS.   ni mi casa es ya mi casa.

*As the sailors' voices fade away your attention comes back to
the crowd on the shore who are still chanting the Litany.
The two longshoremen are looking out to sea.*

VASCO. So that be end of that!
LUÍS. Not a bad start, howsomever.
       They sail better'n I thought.
       Pity the *Niña* got lateen sails.
VASCO. *Pinta* can go a lick though.
LUÍS. Aye, got a lovely run off a fair wind.
       Pretty sight they make surely;
       Wind filling out the sails with a red cross on each of
       'em
       And the sun shining on the gold trucks and the
       taffrail—
            A woman is heard sobbing.
       What be wrong with *you?*
WOMAN. They've taken away my man.
       He's on the *Santa Maria.*
       I'll never see him again.
VASCO. Reckon you won't.
LUÍS. Don't say that, you fool ...
       Stiff ships, bain't they. Look at their wake.
WOMAN. I'll never see him again.
       I'll never see him again.
VASCO. Well, you're not the only one.
BEATRIZ. No, she's not the only one.
VASCO. Beg your pardon, lady. I didn't see you.
       Lady like you oughtn't to be in this crowd.
BEATRIZ. A lady like me oughtn't to be alive.
LUÍS (*humming*)
            La - la - la - la - la ...

[64]

All this unhappiness!
The white horses be happy enough;
Look at 'em leaping at the stem.
BEATRIZ. White horses? The horses of the sea.
The horses of the sea are taking him away.
LUÍS. You don't look well, Señora. You ought to go home.
BEATRIZ. There is no point in my going home.
LUÍS. Any connection of yours sail on them ships?
BEATRIZ. Any connection of mine?
VASCO. He means husband or father or summat.
BEATRIZ. No, my friends. Nothing like that.
It is only someone I used to know—
He's out there now on the poop of the *Santa Maria*
But he is not any connection of mine.
VASCO. Then you're lucky. This poor creature here—
Look how she's a-crying of her eyes out.
BEATRIZ. Poor thing. I almost wish
I could cry my eyes out too—
But that would be out of proportion.
I can hardly see him now, standing there in the
stern;
He thinks he knows where he's going,
He will never know what he's leaving behind.
VASCO. And what may he be leaving behind?
BEATRIZ. Only a woman he does not love . . .
Only that and a child he will never know.
On those ships they are singing.
Singing away in time to their work,
Singing away without ceasing
As if this voyage would go on for ever—
And so it will, so it will;
None of those ships will ever come back.
And the man standing there on the poop—
The father of my child to be—
He too will never come back.
Not in a month of parboiled days,
Not in a year of palsied months,
Not in an age of haunted years—
He won't come back, he won't come back.
Pause.
(*fading*). And all they can do is sing!

[65]

That is what they are doing.
A Hauling Shanty creeps up into the foreground.

SOLO.   We're gone away for ever, for ever on the
               ocean,
CHORUS.   Gone away for ever, for ever and a day,
SOLO.   Gone away for ever, for ever on the ocean,
CHORUS.   Gone away for ever, for ever and a day.

SOLO.   In sunlight and starlight, in springtime and
               autumn
CHORUS.   Gone away for ever, for ever and a day,
SOLO.   In snowfall and nightfall, in darkness and
               downfall
CHORUS.   Gone away for ever, for ever and a day.

SOLO.   Out upon the ocean we're flotsam and jetsam,
CHORUS.   Gone away for ever, for ever and a day,
SOLO.   We're ragtag and bobtail, we're lost and we're
               lonely,
CHORUS.   Gone away for ever, for ever and a day.

From the sailors' voices you move to the captain's cabin.

COLUMBUS (*writing in journal*)
'Friday, August the third, Fourteen-Ninety-Two:
Set sail from the bar of Saltes in Palos at eight o'clock
and proceeded with a strong breeze till sunset, fif-
teen leagues South afterwards South-West and
South by West which is the direction of the
Canaries.'

'September the sixth: Cleared from the Canaries
and sailed due West.'

'September the ninth: Sailed this day nineteen
leagues, and determined to count less than the true
number, that the crew might not be discouraged if
the voyage should prove long. . . .
The sailors steered badly, causing the vessels to fall to
leeward toward the North East, for which the admiral reprimanded them repeatedly.'

[66]

From the captain's cabin you move back to the sailors.

BARTOLOMÉ. Told us off he did. How can *us* help it?

FRANCISCO. That's right. What do he think we are?

BARTOLOMÉ. Damned galley slaves—that's what he thinks we are.

FRANCISCO. Sooner be back in prison.

CARLOS. You know what *I* think? I think he's mad.

FRANCISCO. Reckon you're right. I'll tell 'ee what I saw only last
night it was. I were on watch in the bits and there he
were a-standing up on the forward castle, standing
up there like a statue up on a church—and talking to
himself he was, face didn't seem to move but he
were a-talking to himself—talking right out loud to
the sea and the moon.

Night-music now throws a light on Columbus talking to himself.

COLUMBUS. 'Where shall wisdom be found and where is the
abode of understanding?
God makes the weight for his winds and he weigh-
eth the waters by measure.'
They knew that I was to come.
Isaiah and Esdras and Job and John the Divine—
They knew that I was to come.
And the Roman poet, Seneca, knew it too—
... venient annis
Saecula seris quibus oceanus
Vincula rerum laxet...
'The time will come in a late
Century when the sea
Will loose the knots of fate
And the earth will be opened up
And the rolled map unfurled
And a new sailor sail
To uncover a new world.'
'The time will come...' The time has come already.
There are strange things happening.

The night-music fades away and we are back with the sailors.

[67]

FRANCISCO. See that? Do 'ee see it? Do 'ee see it or don't 'ee?
BARTOLOMÉ. I see it all right. It's just I don't believe it.
FRANCISCO. Hey, Carlos, come and look at this.
CARLOS. Look at what? What's wrong with you?
FRANCISCO. The needle, Carlos, the compass needle,
    The needle, the fly, the lily.
    Come and look at this here lunatic needle.
CARLOS. The needle, Francisco? What's wrong with her?
BARTOLOMÉ. Witchcraft. That's what's wrong with her.
CARLOS. Well. Let's have a look.
FRANCISCO. A moment, Carlos. Tell me—
    You know this magnetic needle—
    What way be she meant to point?
CARLOS. Why, we all know that. She points due North,
    She points to the Stella Maris.
FRANCISCO. Very well, Carlos. Come ye here and see.
                        Pause.
CARLOS. Nombre de Dios!
FRANCISCO. Well, Carlos? What way be she pointing now?
CARLOS. But this is mad. She's swung to the West,
    She's pointing well North West,
    Pointing North West a fourth of the wind.
FRANCISCO. A fourth of the wind, eh? Well, Carlos?
    What do 'ee think of that?
BARTOLOMÉ. It's summat no one's ever heard of.
    Us was wrong to come on this voyage.
FRANCISCO. Wrong! Us was signing our death-warrant.
    Better have taken our twenty years in jail.
    The laws of Man be one thing,
    The laws of Nature be another—
    Way out here in this here empty sea
    The laws of Nature don't work no more;
    Nature—as us knew her—Nature don't exist.
BARTOLOMÉ. 'Tis the Devil that rules out here.
CARLOS. The Devil? I don't know about that—
    But we've got a devil of our own right here on
      board
    And it's him that gives us our orders.
FRANCISCO. He won't be giving us orders not much longer—
    Not if this here sort of thing go on.
BARTOLOMÉ. A sailor's life be a hard life but this beats all.

[68]

FRANCISCO. Nothing from day to day nor week to week
　　　　　　But steel band of horizon
　　　　　　Like a steel collar on your throat;
　　　　　　It make me feel I'm choking.
CARLOS. What does he care if you choke?
　　　　　A man like that who never sleeps a wink,
　　　　　A man like that who talks to himself—
FRANCISCO. And 'tain't as if he only talked to himself.
　　　　　　I've watched him there in the night. He talk a spell
　　　　　　And then he stop and listen.
　　　　　　What do 'ee think he listen to?
CARLOS. Don't ask *me*. I never learned black magic.
FRANCISCO. No, but I tell 'ee; I've seen it—
　　　　　　There he stand listening and listening.
　　　　　　What do 'ee think he listen to?

What do you think?

FAITH. You shall achieve what you have designed—
ECHO. 　　　　　　　　　　you have designed.
DOUBT The steed you are riding is doomed to a fall—
ECHO. 　　　　　　　　　　doomed to a fall.
FAITH. Beyond the horizon is something to find—
ECHO. 　　　　　　　　　　something to find.
DOUBT. Beyond the horizon is nothing at all—
　　　　　　　　　　　　nothing at all.

FAITH. Your name is Christopher, Bearer of Christ—
ECHO. 　　　　　　　　　　Bearer of Christ.
DOUBT. You are the Dove that cannot get free—
ECHO. 　　　　　　　　　　cannot get free.
FAITH. What you shall find is a world unpriced—
ECHO. 　　　　　　　　　　a world unpriced.
DOUBT. What you are seeking is lost in the sea—
　　　　　　　　　　　　lost in the sea.

FAITH. Forward and follow the star in your mind—
ECHO. 　　　　　　　　　　star in your mind.
DOUBT. Better turn back or worse will befall—
ECHO. 　　　　　　　　　　worse will befall.
FAITH. Beyond the horizon is something to find—
ECHO. 　　　　　　　　　　something to find.

DOUBT. Beyond the horizon is nothing at all—
nothing at all.
COLUMBUS. Nothing at all? That is not true,
For the last few days there have been signs.
Floating grasses, a live crab—
Never found beyond eighty leagues of land;
A whale—whales are always near the land;
A floating branch with berries—that means land
too,
And those white birds flying south-west—
Where could they be going if not to land?
Land ... land ... land ...
FAITH. Land is ahead, so be not depressed—
ECHO. be not depressed.
DOUBT. All is mirage. Disappointment is all—
ECHO. disappointment is all.
FAITH. Keep on your course. There is land in the West—
land in the West.
DOUBT. Better turn back or worse will befall—
worse will befall.
COLUMBUS. Better turn back? Turn back!
Who dares tell me that?
Man—or more than man—who dares use those words?
SPOKESMAN OF CREW.
Turn back, Captain, turn back.
COLUMBUS. What's that? Who said that?
SPOKESMAN OF CREW.
'Turn back, Captain.' I said that.
I am the spokesman of your crew.
We have gone as long as we can.
We cannot go on any more.
COLUMBUS. Indeed, Señor?
You say you speak for the crew.
I do not believe you.
SPOKESMAN OF CREW.
You don't believe me? Look out on the deck.
COLUMBUS. You're a mutineer. I'll put you in irons.
SPOKESMAN OF CREW.
You can't put us all in irons.
Look out on the deck, I tell you.
Murmurs from the crew.

[70]

COLUMBUS. What are the fools doing? Why are they not at their
　　　　posts?
　　　　Hallo there! Why are you not at your posts?
VOICE (*distant*).
　　　　Because we want an answer.
COLUMBUS. Answer to what, you fools?
VOICE (*distant*)
　　　　Will you turn back—or won't you?
CREW (*chanting*). We want to go back.
　　　　　　　We want to go back.
　　　　　　　We want to go back.
SPOKESMAN OF CREW.
　　　　You see, Captain?
COLUMBUS. I see.
　　　　I will have a few words with this scum.
CREW (*Nearer and Crescendo*).
　　　　　　　We want to go back.
　　　　　　　We want to go back.
　　　　　　　We want to go back.
COLUMBUS. Silence there!
　　　　So you want to go back?
　　　　You disappoint me, gentlemen.
　　　　Don't you know our voyage is nearly done?
　　　　We are within a few days' sail of land.
VOICE. Who says so?
COLUMBUS. I say so, my friend. I have seen the signs.
VOICE. Signs!
　　　　　　Murmurs from the crew.
COLUMBUS. All last night I heard—and so did you—
　　　　All last night we heard birds passing
　　　　Flying West South West.
　　　　That means land.
1ST VOICE. I don't believe it.'
2ND VOICE. Why should it mean land?
COLUMBUS. You fool! What else could it mean?
2ND VOICE. I'll tell you what it could mean.
　　　　Back in the seas of Europe birds are a sign of land
　　　　But away out here on the rimless rim of the world
　　　　Things are different, signs are no longer signs,
　　　　And birds are no longer birds. How do we know
　　　　These birds that pass in the night are not a trick

Of the Devil to lead us on
To one mirage of land after another
Until our food is gone and our ship falls to pieces
And we ourselves are madmen, drowned in a mad
sea?
1ST VOICE. He's right, Captain, he's right.
We've gone as far as we can. It's time to turn back.
CREW. We want to go back.
We want to go back.
WE WANT TO GO BACK.
COLUMBUS. Silence, you knock-kneed trash. You're wasting
your time.
I am Christopher Columbus. I do *not* turn back.
2ND VOICE. Oh yes you will, if we say so.
1ST VOICE. If you won't yield to reason, you'll yield to force.
SPOKESMAN OF CREW.
He's right, Captain. You can't keep on
If all your crew are against you.
COLUMBUS. I know that. Keep quiet.
Listen to me, Señores,
Today is October the eighth; it is my reckoning
We shall strike land within three days. Give me
five—
If by then the land has failed us,
Then we shall reconsider what we must do.
Only wait five days. I know it in my heart
That land is over there. Señor Pinzón,
Captain of the *Pinta*, thinks so too—
And he, as you know, is a master seaman,
Well, Señores, if he and I are right,
All your troubles are over. What remains is glory—
Glory, my friends, and gold. We have good reason
To think that over there there is gold in plenty,
Just beyond the horizon. The land out there—
The land to which those white birds keep flying—
Is a land where gold flows in the streams, where
gold
Drips from the trees, where gold
Litters the shores and lies pell-mell in the fields.
Gold, señores, gold...
Gold, gold, gold, gold.

CREW (*whispering*).
    Gold ... gold ... gold ...
    Gold ... gold ... gold ...
COLUMBUS. Give me five days more.
CREW (*Louder*).
    Gold, gold, gold, gold,
    Gold, gold, gold, gold ...
COLUMBUS. Give me five days more.
CREW (*Loud and crescendo*)
    Gold, gold, gold, gold, gold,
    Gold, gold, gold, gold, GOLD.
VOICE. Captain!
COLUMBUS. Yes?
VOICE. We will go on.
CREW (*to themselves*).
    Gold ... gold ... gold ... gold ...

*When their murmuring has faded away Columbus is heard
making another entry in his diary.*

COLUMBUS. 'October the eleventh: This day the *Pinta* picked up
a reed and a stick, and another stick carved, as it
seemed, with iron tools . . . and some grass which
grows on land . . . and a tablet of wood. The crew
on seeing these signs breathed and felt great joy!'

BARTOLOMÉ. Hear what the *Pinta* found today?
FRANCISCO. Course I heard. Things be lookin' up.
BARTOLOMÉ. Captain's ordered a special watch. First as sights
land, he'll get a rare reward.
FRANCISCO. What be time now?
BARTOLOMÉ. Near two hours till midnight. Dark night bain't it?
FRANCISCO. Ssh! Here comes Captain.
       Pause.
COLUMBUS. All correct here?
BARTOLOMÉ. All correct, Captain.
COLUMBUS. Either of you seen anything?
BARTOLOMÉ.⎫
      ⎬No, Captain, nothing.
FRANCISCO.⎭

COLUMBUS. Keep your eyes skinned.
What's that yonder?
BARTOLOMÉ. What, Captain?
FRANCISCO. I can't see nothing.
COLUMBUS. That little light.
FRANCISCO. Light?
BARTOLOMÉ. Light?
COLUMBUS. You're blind, you fools, you're blind.
Where's Pedro Gutiérrez? *He's* got eyes.
FRANCISCO. I'll fetch him for 'ee, Captain.
COLUMBUS. Light, of course it's a light . . . But it comes and goes,
Like a taper of wax rising and falling—
BARTOLOMÉ. Maybe it's just a star.
COLUMBUS. Star, you fool?
Who ever saw a star moving from side to side
Dipping and jerking? This—
If it's not an illusion—this is a sign of life,
This is a sign of land—
FRANCISCO. Here 'ee be, Captain.
Here's Gutiérrez, and Rodrigo Sánchez too—
Another fellow with gimlet eyes.
COLUMBUS. Come here, Gutiérrez. And you too, Sánchez.
Look over there where I point.
What do you see, Gutiérrez?
GUTIÉRREZ. Where, Captain? I see nothing.
COLUMBUS. Look where I'm pointing, damn you. Don't you see
a light?
No it's gone out now. Wait.
Keep your eyes over there.
GUTIÉRREZ. Right, Captain. I'm waiting.
COLUMBUS. Now! Do you see it?
GUTIÉRREZ. No.
COLUMBUS. It's gone out again. Keep looking.
Now!
GUTIÉRREZ. Where? Where? . . . Mother of God!
Yes, I see it.
Yes, it *is* a light. A light.
COLUMBUS. And you, Sánchez, do you see it?
SÁNCHEZ. Can't say as I do.
COLUMBUS. Don't you see any light?
SÁNCHEZ. Nay, Captain. Can't see nothing.

COLUMBUS. But you must. You must see it, you must.
SÁNCHEZ. Nay, Captain, I don't.
COLUMBUS. But you see it, don't you, Gutiérrez?
GUTIÉRREZ. I see it surely. By God I see it.
COLUMBUS. Then it is land at last.
FRANCISCO. That's what *he* says.
BARTOLOMÉ. Reckon he's right. It's land.
FRANCISCO. Sánchez don't see it.
BARTOLOMÉ. No, but Gutiérrez do.
FRANCISCO. Well, we shall know at dawn.
COLUMBUS. Stand by for the dawn!

CHORUS. Look... Look... Look!
What do we see in the dawn?
What do we see in the dawn?
DOUBT. You see a mirage like many before;
A misty shape that is merely mist.
CHORUS. No... No... No!
It is something else we see.
What can it be we see?
FAITH. You see what you have sailed to find.
You see what none has found before.
CHORUS. Land... Land... Land!
Taking shape in the rising sun,
A green land with a golden beach,
A land of colour, a land of life,
A land, a land, a land!

The Te Deum *swells up from the decks of the ships and mingles with the chanting of the Indians on the shore.*

BARTOLOMÉ. Look 'ee yonder. Look on the shore.
What be they on shore?
What in God's name be *they*?
FRANCISCO. Yon be living men.
Ask Gutiérrez here,
Hey, Gutiérrez, you have eyes like a needle.
Yon things moving on the island—
Tell us if they be men.

[75]

GUTIÉRREZ. Of course they're men. Wait and I'll describe them.
They're moving down to the bay from the green
hill—
A whole crowd of naked men and women
Bronze in colour, lithe as gazelles,
They've feathers on their heads, they're jumping
From rock to rock like goats;
Here they come now, down to the frills of the surf,
They're gathering there in their ranks, they're lifting
their arms to the sky,
And bowing themselves to the sand; I cannot hear a
sound
But it looks as if they're singing or praying,
I think they're singing or praying ...

INDIAN CHORUS. Guanahani! Guanahani!
LEADER. Who come now to Guanahani?
CHORUS. Over sea. Over sea.
LEADER. The gods are come from over sea.
CHORUS. The gods are come to Guanahani.

INDIAN CHORUS. Guanahani! Guanahani!
LEADER. From the birthplace of the sun,
CHORUS. With the sun to Guanahani,
LEADER. Come the children of the sun,
CHORUS. White gods to Guanahani.

INDIAN CHORUS. To the shore of Guanahani
LEADER. Here they come, here they come,
CHORUS. Here they come to Guanahani,
LEADER. The white gods are come, are come,
CHORUS. To the shore of Guanahani.
The Spaniards are now wading ashore through the surf.

INDIAN CHORUS. Guanahani! Guanahani!
LEADER. Stepping through the silver foam
CHORUS. On the sands of Guanahani
LEADER. Come the shining sons of Heaven
CHORUS. To our land of Guanahani.

INDIAN CHORUS. Guanahani! Guanahani!
    LEADER. Let us pray. Let us pray.
    CHORUS. Pray! Pray! Pray! Pray!
    LEADER. To these gods who step ashore,
    CHORUS. Step ashore on Guanahani.
    The Spaniards are now drawn up on the beach.

COLUMBUS. Are you here, Martín Pinzón, Captain of the *Pinta?*
MARTIN PINZÓN.
    Aye, my Lord Admiral.
COLUMBUS. And you, Vicente Pinzón, Captain of the *Nina?*
VICENTE PINZÓN.
    Aye, my Lord Admiral.
COLUMBUS. And you, Rodrigo de Segovia, Inspector of the Fleet?
SEGOVIA. Aye, my Lord Admiral.
COLUMBUS. Good. Stand by and take note.
    Fanfare.
    In the name of the Holy Trinity
    I here upon this hitherto heathen land—
    In the year of Our Lord Fourteen Hundred and
        Ninety-two
    And the twelfth day of October—
    Erect the cross of Christ.
    CHORUS. Per Dominum!
COLUMBUS. And in the name of their Catholic Majesties
    I raise the banner of Castile.
    And I thus take over this island in the name of their
        Catholic majesties.
    Señor de Escovedo, enter the same in your record.
ESCOVEDO. I will, my Lord Admiral.
COLUMBUS. And I hereby name this island . . .
    San Salvador.
    CHORUS. Per Dominum! Per Dominum! Per Dominum!
COLUMBUS. And I now instruct you all:
    You see this island—it is like the garden of Eden,
    And you see its naked inhabitants
    Who are like Adam and Eve, knowing not good or
        evil.
    Here they lie on their faces before us,
    Grovelling to us as gods.
    It is for us to teach them good,

It is for us to save them from evil.
Therefore, Señores, in this new world
Conduct yourselves as worthy sons of Spain
And true servants of Christ.
CHORUS. We will, Señor, we will!

INDIAN CHORUS. (*Mid-distance*).
                    Guanahani! Guanahani!
    LEADER. These are gods. These are gods.
    CHORUS. These are gods in Guanahani.
    LEADER. They have come but they will go,
    CHORUS. Go again from Guanahani.

COLUMBUS. Señor de Escovedo.
ESCOVEDO. Here my Lord Admiral.
COLUMBUS. You are to keep a full record of all my proceedings
          here;
          Leave no chink for the fingers of malice.
          I intend to explore this island and all the lands
          adjacent,
          Discovering all they contain of interest or treasure
          And making a report of the same for Her Majesty
          Queen Isabella.
ESCOVEDO. Yes, my Lord Admiral.
COLUMBUS. This part of the world, as you can see, is rich—
          Blessed with the bounty of God in plants and
          precious stones,
          Cinnamon, musk and aloes and who knows what?
          I also expect gold—
          You have seen the gold rings they wear in their
          noses—
          But more important than that,
          More important than this or the next door island
          Is the continent lying beyond us,
          The realm of the Great Khan.
          We are now on the fringe of Asia.
ESCOVEDO. You think so, my Lord Admiral?
COLUMBUS. I know so. Why! If we are not near Asia,
          Where in the round world are we?
ESCOVEDO. I couldn't tell you. I have never been here.
          It only occurred to me that between Europe and
          Asia

There might be something else.

COLUMBUS. And so there is, Señor. There is this island
And many another like it.
These are the islands which Marco Polo spoke of;
One of them is Zipangu.

ESCOVEDO. I was not thinking of islands—
Or not, at least, of Marco Polo's islands.
I was thinking that maybe—maybe, my Lord
Admiral—
We may have struck a new mainland.

COLUMBUS. Señor de Escovedo, you are my notary.
You are not a cosmographer.
I tell you, Señor, what we have done
Is to find the western passage to Asia;
This island on which we stand is off the shore of
Asia.

ESCOVEDO. You know best, my Lord Admiral.

COLUMBUS. That being so, since we know where we stand,
My plan of action is this:
I shall remain here but a couple of months,
Exploring, collecting, recording.
Then I shall sail for home with the news—
'News', Señor! The word is too weak;
What I shall tell them in Spain is more than news,
it's a gospel—
The epilogue to the previous history of Man,
The prelude to his future.

ESCOVEDO. Yes, my lord Admiral.
So we shall sail for home?

COLUMBUS. We shall, Señor. In two or three months from
now.

*The Indian song comes up again and covers Columbus'
departure for Europe.*

INDIAN CHORUS. Guanahani! Guanahani!
    LEADER. The white gods have left the shore.
    CHORUS. Left the shore of Guanahani,
    LEADER. Gone again into the sunrise,
    CHORUS. Gone again from Guanahani

*The Indian voices fade into nothing; this nothing resolves to
the shore of Europe.*

HIDALGO. What are you doing there, fellow?

PEASANT. Eh?

HIDALGO. What are you doing perched up there on that rock
Straining your eyes on the sea?
I've been watching you, my man;
You've been stuck up there an hour.

PEASANT. I've been stuck up here for weeks.

HIDALGO. What for, my man, what for?

PEASANT. I'm keeping a look-out.

HIDALGO. A look-out?

PEASANT. Aye, I come from Cordoba.

HIDALGO. Cordoba? What's that got to do with it?

PEASANT. 'Twas a lady in Cordoba sent me here.
She told me for to keep look-out.

HIDALGO. Stop talking like an idiot.
What did this lady in Cordoba send you here to look
out for?

PEASANT. Why, for Señor Columbus.

HIDALGO. Señor . . .? Nombre de Dios!
You mean Columbus that sailed to the West last
year?

PEASANT. Aye, that be the one.

HIDALGO. And you mean to say you're sitting here
Day after day, week after week,
Waiting for *him*! You're mad,
As mad as Columbus himself.

PEASANT. Doña Beatriz—she had a dream.

HIDALGO. A dream! She must have had several.
Your Señor Columbus will never come back to
Spain.
We all knew that when he sailed.

PEASANT. No matter. I keep my look-out.
The lady in Cordoba pays me.

HIDALGO. I hope she pays you well.
Columbus, you see, will never come back to
Europe.
Columbus will never come back—not in a thousand
years.

[80]

Music answers back the hidalgo and prepares you for the Return.

VASCO. Heard the news?
LUÍS. What news, Vasco?
VASCO. Columbus be back.
LUÍS. *Who* be back?
VASCO. Columbus. Christopher Columbus. He just put into
    port.

PRIOR. Heard the news, Brother Antonio?
ANTONIO. What news, Father Prior?
PRIOR. Our friend Columbus is back. He has found his land
    in the West.
ANTONIO. I always knew he would. Thank God!
PRIOR. Thank God!

CLERIC. Have you heard the news, Your Grace?
TALAVERA. What news, Señor?
CLERIC. Christopher Columbus has arrived in Palos.
TALAVERA. I do not believe it, Señor.
CLERIC. And what is more, he has found his land in the West.
TALAVERA. I tell you, I do not believe it.

WAITING WOMAN.
    Doña Beatriz! Doña Beatriz!
BEATRIZ. Yes, what is it?
WAITING WOMAN.
    Have you heard the news?
BEATRIZ. Yes, Maria, I have.
             Pause.
    I heard it before anyone.
WAITING WOMAN.
    And what are you going to do?
BEATRIZ. Do, Maria? Nothing.
             Pause.
    If he comes through Cordoba perhaps I will watch
    from the window.

ISABELLA. Heard the news, Marquesa?

MARQUESA. What news, Your Majesty?

ISABELLA. Columbus has come back.

MARQUESA. Columbus has come back!

ISABELLA. Yes, my friend, and he's found it.

MARQUESA. Found . . . *it?*

ISABELLA. Found what we hoped he would. God is great.

MARQUESA. And where is Columbus now?

ISABELLA. In Seville. Waiting instructions.

MARQUESA. Then he will come to the Court?
He will come here to Barcelona?

ISABELLA. Yes, he will come to Barcelona.

Processional music anticipates the procession.

ONLOOKER. Here they come now, here they come now,
The long procession leaving the gates of Seville,
En route for Barcelona.
Have a good look, ladies and gentlemen, never again
Will this city of Seville see such a wild to-do.
Look at the shining soldiers bearing coffers of gold,
Look at the tattered banners bleached with the brine,
Look at the red savages crowned with feathers—
Gold rings in their noses and popinjays on their shoulders—
Look at the golden masks, the pearls and mother of pearl,
And look at who comes here—the Discoverer himself,
The man who is now the talk of Europe, the Very Magnificent Lord
Admiral of the Ocean Sea, Viceroy of the Western World,
With his pale face and his burning eyes, sitting his horse
Like a Roman Emperor . . . or
It might be fitter to say like the fifth
Horseman of the Apocalypse.

The procession draws level.
Columbus' followers are chanting in the manner of a Round.

Back from the West

Beyond the world
Back from the West

We have returned
Beyond the world
Back from the West

And here we are
We have returned
Beyond the world
Back from the West

And here we are
We have returned
Beyond the world

And here we are
We have returned

And here we are!

ALL TOGETHER.　Back from the West
Beyond the world
We have returned
And here we are.

SPOKESMAN OF PROCESSION.
From Seville over the Sierras, bound for the Royal
Court,
By a dusty road to the banks of the Guadalquivir,
To a Moorish city of winding streets and gardens
Set among groves of olive and orange,
Here we come in our Admiral's train
Bearing the wealth of the West and the news of the
Indies
Here we come to Cordoba, here
Through Cordoba we come riding.

*As the cheers of the onlookers recede you notice Doña Beatriz
in a balcony.*

WAITING WOMAN.
        Doña Beatriz! Doña Beatriz! Did you see him?
BEATRIZ. Yes, but he didn't see *me*.
        He rode by in the way that he would—
        Looking neither to right nor to left.
WAITING WOMAN.
        This is a day for him!
        A day of triumph.
BEATRIZ. A day—I would say—of miracle.
        But he will die unhappy.

*The music surges back, Beatriz is left behind and we ride on
with Columbus.*

SPOKESMAN OF PROCESSION.
        From Cordoba we go on, from Cordoba to
            Montoro,
        From Montoro to Jaén huddled on wooded hills,
        From Jaén to Orihuela on the banks of the Segura
        And thence to Alicante with its palm-trees by the
            sea,
        And everywhere the crowds come out to meet us
            and they throw
        Flowers upon our heads and we ride on
        With our Indians and our popinjays and gold;
        We ride on, ride on.
CHORUS.   Back from the West
            Beyond the world
            We have returned
            And here we are.
SPOKESMAN OF PROCESSION.
        And now we come to the great white port of
            Valencia
        With its multitude of roofs and its towering
            campanile
        And the people of Valencia bring us flowers and
            bring us fruit,

Blow us kisses as we were lovers and look up to us
as gods—
And we smile the smile of gods and we ride on.
And we come to Catalunya, to Roman Tarragona,
With its dark cobbled alleys clambering up the hill
And the smell of fish and wine
And the broken Roman arches that betoken
So much glory of the past
Which is nothing to the glory that is ours
That surrounds us as we ride to the King and Queen
of Spain
Holding court in Barcelona . . .
HERALD. Holding court in Barcelona!

*The processional music ends and silence introduces the Court
at Barcelona.*

ISABELLA. Señor Don Christopher Columbus!
We Isabella, Queen of Castile and Aragon,
Do here before the assembled peers of our land
Welcome you back to Spain and give you our royal
thanks
For that against the odds you have done what you
have done
To the greater glory of God and the honour of
Spain.
Of your achievements we have already heard
And here we see their tangible evidence—
The gold, the pearls, and these strange men;
But we ask you now, Señor, out of your own
mouth
Here to address the Crown and the Peers of Spain—
Aye, and the whole of the serried Christian world—
And tell us your own story and what it means.
COLUMBUS. Your Catholic Majesties . . . it is hard for me
On such a day and before such an audience,
Feeling myself on a pinnacle high among clouds of
dream,
To find the words—it is hard to find the words

[85]

For a theme that no man yet has phrased or
    painted—
The passage where no passage lay,
The world where no world was before.
But this is what I have done:
I took three ships and sailed them into the teeth of
    the West,
Into what seemed the certainty of death
And against the veto of Nature.
Weeks went by and no land came, I might have
Well turned back but I did not. I went on
And in the ripeness of God's will I found
The second Earthly Paradise and there
I raised the cross of Christ and the banner of
    Castile.
Your Majesties, look out yonder,
Look out yonder along the line of my arm
Across Tibidabo and the hills of Spain:
Four thousand miles out there to the West
Lie uncharted lands—they are yours to chart,
Uncounted treasure—yours for the taking,
Aye and countless hordes of heathen men
Who are from now your subjects,
Unenlightened souls who wait the light.
Aye, your Majesties, this new world
That I have opened up through the will of God—
Only God can tell what is its total worth,
And God alone knows what it will become
Or what may be the blessings that late or soon
May flow from thence to Europe—
Aye, and to all mankind from this new world.
This is my story and this is what it means:
Here and now at your court in Barcelona
In the year of Our Lord Fourteen-Hundred-And-
    Ninety-Three,
Before the Throne of Spain and the eyes and ears of
    Europe
And before the crowded jury of posterity—
I have brought you a new world.

    The crowd then sing in triumph.

LEADER.   Glory, glory to God.
             Joy in the land of Spain.
             They sailed away to the West,
             Now they are here again.

CHORUS.   Glory, glory to God.
             Joy in the land of Spain.

LEADER.   They sailed away to the West,
             Now they are here again.
             They tracked the sun to his lair,
             They found the Golden Main.

CHORUS.   They sailed away to the West,
             Now they are here again.
COLUMBUS (*calling from distance*).
             I have brought you a new world.

LEADER.   The world that we have found
             Shall ne'er be lost again.
             The voyage that we made—
             We made it not in vain.

CHORUS.   The world that we have found
             Shall ne'er be lost again.

APPENDIX

Christopher Columbus is a radio-drama written to order and with a special end in view. After its first transmission on October 12th, 1942, a radio critic complained that I had ended the story with Columbus' triumphant return to Spain after the discovery instead of extending it to include his unfortunate later voyages and the poignant record of his decline and fall; another critic was obsessed by the thought that Christopher Marlowe would have made the verse much more heroic. My answers to these two intelligent but amateur criticisms should be foreseen from the Introduction to this book.

(*a*) Construction and 'over-all' unity being in a radio play of primary importance, a heroic subject, such as the discovery of America, required an epic rather than a psychological treatment. The later career of Columbus, though vastly interesting from a biographical angle, would by transferring interest from the *muthos* to the character (i.e. to the character not only as distinct from but as opposed to the *muthos*), have broken the programme in two, confused the listener and given him possibly a feeling of anti-climax.[1] This programme, moreover, was intended to cele- brate the 450th anniversary of the discovery of America; in writing an anniversary programme for the Battle of Waterloo I would not include that picture from 1833 of Wellington in Apsley House— the duchess lying dead inside while the mob is breaking the windows. Similarly, with *Alexander Nevsky*, neither Eisenstein's film nor my radio adaptation of it was bothered by the fact that Nevsky spent his later years appeasing the Tartars.

(*b*) Marlowe as a radio-dramatist? He might have made a very good one but he would have had to loosen his verse; the verse of *Tamburlaine*, within a few years of its writing, became too stiff, too pompous and monotonous, even for the stage of the day (witness Shakespeare's parodies of it). In our twentieth century at any rate dramatic verse—whether for the stage or the air—must be flexible enough to fit a wide diversity of characters and to move from the heights to the flats without an obvious change of tech- nique such as Shakespeare's breaks into prose; a stage-play that shows this flexibility is Mr. Eliot's *Family Reunion*. Radio espec-

[1] Such an anti-climax would be much more feasible on the stage where one gambles on a sophisticated audience.

ially should avoid a sustained metronomic beat which would march into the listener's parlour like a platoon of guardsmen. In *Christopher Columbus*, therefore, I used for the dialogue an irregular blank verse based upon the rhythms of ordinary speech but capable of being heightened or tightened, flattened or bepurpled to requirements.[1] The lyrics on the other hand I wrote in a regular form and made very simple in sentence structure and imagery because they were designed to be sung or, in some cases, spoken against music. I take it as a compliment that both the composer and actors seemed to think I had played into their hands.

Christopher Columbus is an untypical radio play (by which I mean play written specially for radio) both because it is so long and because it involved so much music, and particularly vocal music. I have decided not to indicate all the places in the text where music was used but, as an example of its importance, I can point out that the whole of Columbus' triumphant procession from Seville to Barcelona had processional music in the background; this meant that the running commentaries in verse during these sequences were delivered, over the music, with much the same tempo and punch that characterise a real running commentary delivered over the noise of a crowd on a sportsground. William Walton's music, I should add, served its purpose admirably; i.e. it was structural.

The vocal interludes require an additional comment from a literary angle. The work as a whole being a stylised treatment of a simple heroic theme, these interludes served some of the same purposes as the choruses in a Greek tragedy. It will be noticed that the two verse-speakers and the two semi-choruses are neither characters nor, in the ordinary sense, narrators[2] but are the mouthpieces of two opposed principles, doubt and faith—a projection as it were of Columbus' inner dialectic; being thus projected outside the protagonist, they allowed me to keep him as simple and wedgelike as I wanted.

[1] For those who are not practitioners and who might consider the above a cover-up for laziness, I would point out that nothing is easier than to write sustained blank verse on the strict heroic beat.

[2] The radio convention of the Narrator seems to me often abused when used, as it is commonly used, merely to convey information; information can usually be conveyed through the mouths of the characters proper; the chief virtue of a Narrator is that like a Greek chorus, he can shake himself free of realism and speak—if needed, in an unrealistic manner—to heighten an emotion or point a moral or suggest a historical perspective.

Since *Christopher Columbus* is so long, the sequences too are unusually long and the build unusually leisurely. It therefore looks more 'literary' than most radio scripts while it lacks those surprises and twists which, in a script of normal length, are often required to make a point in a flash—a dynamic *multum in parvo*. I rather regret the absence of such tricks but the tempo of the work did not require them and they might have conflicted with the one-way dignity of the theme. The temptation to stunt in this way might also have involved the wider temptation to debunk the Columbus legend. Columbus, a man who like Hitler relied on his intuitions and was rather an offensive character, should after all be a godsend to those who enjoy debunking. My concern, however, was first with the Discovery and then with the Discoverer with a capital D. The small d, the small columbus, could be shelved.

This brings me to the question of history. Columbus became a legend first in his own mind, and to all romantics since. Radio drama, like all other forms of drama, being primarily directed to the emotions, my first object was to retain the *emotional* truth preserved in the legend rather than to let it dissolve in a maelstrom of historical details. On the other hand, in treating such a very *historical* event as the discovery of America, I did not consider myself entitled to alter the main outlines of the discovery and what led up to it or to misrepresent—except by simplification—the character of the discoverer *qua* discoverer. One thing that seems to be agreed about Columbus is that, whether or not he was a first-class navigator, he was a man of one idea with an almost mystical faith in his mission. This is how I have tried to portray him.

It should be remembered that many of the 'facts' about Columbus are still open to controversy. The following Notes will make some historical points which may not be clear in history or in the script. It will be seen that, for dramatic reasons, I have done some minor transpositions and made some minor exaggerations. In the same way I have throughout used the name Christopher Columbus; he was of course Cristóbal Colón.

NOTES

Page 22. *The King of Portugal* at the time was John II. The Portuguese were then the world's champion explorers but Columbus' proposals were apparently too vague for their liking. He wrote many years later that the Lord shut the King's eyes and ears and all his senses to the truth.

Page 26. *Antonio de Marchena* was not, I believe, present at La Rabida when Columbus arrived there. However, I required his presence.

Page 27. *That the world is a sphere* was, contrary to popular tradition since, generally admitted at this date by educated persons. Globes were already in use but the Tripartite World was commonly thought of as on *top* of the globe. It was therefore the fear of getting *under* the world that deterred would-be circumnavigators.

Page 36. *The Marquesa's song* I wrote as a deliberate pastiche of fifteenth century Spanish Romance poetry.

Page 39. *The Royal Commission* did exist and did reject Columbus' proposals but there seems to be some doubt as to where it met and how often and under whose presidency. I have ignored these doubts. I have also presented Talavera and the Commission more as Columbus saw them than as they really were.

Page 47. *Beatriz Enríquez* gave offence to some radio critics who, if they did not assume that I had invented her, tended to complain that this *affaire* was inconsistent with Columbus' character. She was in fact the mother of Columbus' son, Fernando Colón (though I have post-dated his birth), but little more is known of her. I introduced her not to modify but to emphasise her lover's single-mindedness.

Page 55. *Luís de Santangel*, apart from making a loan to Isabella, seems largely to have been responsible for her consenting to Columbus' expedition. In a more psychological treatment of this story he should feature quite largely, as should Ferdinand.

Page 59. *The signing-on of jailbirds* is a stock part of the Columbus legend and may be mainly, or merely, legend. I retained it for its wider truth—that most great projects are achieved through the use of unlikely instruments.

Page 59. *Martín Pinzón* is another figure whom I have not given his historical due. In any play which concentrates on the First Voyage itself he might well be the deuteragonist.

Page 63. *The double refrain* of this shanty is taken from a poem by Lorca and means: 'Because I am not (any longer) I and my house is not my house.'

Page 67. *This quotation* from Seneca's *Medea* was translated by Columbus himself in his *Book of Prophecies* (written in 1501 A.D.).

Page 74. *The sighting of land* is another disputed point. The tradition is that, while Pedro Gutiérrez was the man who established the light, one Rodrigo de Triana (or Juan Rodriguez Bermejo) was the first to see the land itself. In any case Columbus himself pocketed the promised reward.

Page 77. *The identity of this island* is still uncertain and it is not agreed by all that Columbus named it San Salvador.

Page 86. *A new world* is a phrase that Columbus would probably not have used. But what else was it?

Addenda

(1) *Cuts:*—This printed version includes some passages—e.g. the list of titles on page 57—which were cut in the radio transmission and probably ought to be cut in any repeat performance. I have printed them here for the fun of it.

(2) *Religion:*—Not being a Roman Catholic, I have not dared to dwell more than a little on that aspect of this story which for a writer like Paul Claudel is the primary one and which most probably must be treated as primary by anyone who hopes to create out of this subject a major work of art.